The Wit & Wisdom of Bob Edwards

The Wit & Wisdom of Bob Edwards

Edited by Hugh Dempsey

with a number of drawings by David Shaw

Hurtig Publishers
Edmonton

Hurtig Publishers
10560 105 Street
Edmonton, Alberta

ISBN 0-88830-120-0 (paper)
ISBN 0-88830-112-X (cloth)

Printed and bound in Canada

Introduction

Robert Chambers ("Bob") Edwards, the irascible editor of the Calgary *Eye Opener* from 1902 to 1922, was one of Canada's most distinctive journalists. A man with a social conscience and a keen wit, he used his "semi-occasional" newspaper to attack the crooked politicians, sanctimonious preachers and social snobs of his day. To accomplish his goals, he used the deadliest weapon in his vast array of literary abilities — humour.

How could any politician respond to this jibe: "We understand — ha ha! — that — haw haw! — R. J. Stuart — ah-yaw-haw — ha ha ha! — is going to run — oh oh ha ha — for alderman — ha ha ha ha ha ha! — Ha ha ha ha ha ha — ha ha ha ha ha ha ha ha ha!"[1]

Or the man of God: "Rev. Kerby disapproves of Sunday golf, eh? Well, what of it? Who cares? We don't."[2]

Or the lawyer: "We always knew that E. P. Davis, of Vancouver, was daffy, though perhaps not daffy enough to be confined in a sanatorium, but we did not think he was one of those who would be guilty of ingratitude. It appears that after his pet frog had consumed all the flies in his house this summer, Davis killed him last week for his legs. This is the limit."[3]

Yet the lampooning of real people was only one part of Edwards's attack on Canadian society. His hard hitting editorials, exposures of political scandals, and his eloquent appeals on behalf of rape victims, working girls, farm labourers and prostitutes made him one of the most widely read journalists of his day. Quoted in newspapers and magazines all across

Canada, as well as in Britain and the United States, he was a tireless crusader on behalf of the "little man."

While collecting material for my earlier book, *The Best of Bob Edwards* (Hurtig Publishers, Edmonton, 1975), I tried to find a balance between Edwards's excellent journalism, fine writing style, humour, and philosophy. I wanted, once and for all, to shatter the myth that Bob Edwards was simply a funny man. Rather, a good cross section of his writing revealed him to be a serious social crusader who was far ahead of his time in matters of law reform, divorce, Canadian nationalism, and morality. Humour was his weapon, both to demolish an enemy and to lull the reader into a receptive mood to receive Edwards's incisive comments.

This volume takes another look at Canada's gifted journalist, this time examining three distinct parts of his writing — his philosophical aphorisms, his popular "society notes," and his jokes. Each had a highly specialized role to play in the twenty-year life of the *Eye Opener*.

Webster's describes an aphorism as "a detached sentence containing some important truth" or a "precept or principle expressed in a few words." This is not a definition which fits some of Edwards's earliest one-liners. Rather, his true aphorisms seem to have gradually evolved over a period of years, almost as a reflection of the author's shifting role from firebrand crusader to mellow humourist.

His writings from 1898 to 1902 in the Wetaskiwin *Free Lance, Alberta Sun,* and Wetaskiwin *Breeze* made use of one-line sentences only as literary devices to draw attention to a particular point he wanted to make in a lengthy article. Often such punch lines appeared at the end of his story, as in a 1898 account which told of the problems of farmers being disappointed by grain buyers and ending with "thus do the summer roses fade."[4]

His early years as editor of the *Eye Opener* saw a gradual shift to one-line phrases which were more humorous than philosophical. A 1905 example, "Endue our ministers with righteousness, O Lord, and make thy chosen people less bughouse."[5] At the same time, the odd aphorism did appear, such as the comment, "No man particularly admires a woman who is so good that all her women acquaintances like her."[6]

The real change in Edwards's writing style occurred between 1908 and 1910, after his humiliating chastisement by a Calgary jury in the McGillicuddy lawsuit, and his subsequent wanderings to Port Arthur and Winnipeg.[7] By the time he returned to Calgary, he had lost much of his vitriolic fire and turned more to humour as a means of political invective.

The first of a steady stream of aphorisms began to appear in the *Eye Opener* in 1910, and were so well received that within two years they had become a regular feature. While at first, many of his one-liners were mixtures of philosophy and political comments, over the years the literary challenge of a skillful aphorism seemed to supplant the sarcastic slash at an enemy's jugular vein.

In 1910, for example, Edwards commented, "Two-thirds of all a man's troubles wear petticoats";[8] "Misfortunes often put us wise to our own carelessness";[9] and, "Any man who can't remember when he was a fool is one yet."[10] By the late teens and early 1920s, many of his aphorisms had become sophisticated gems: "Conscience is a watchdog that barks at sin";[11] "In this world of strife a man must be either an anvil or a hammer";[12] "Too many salt away money in the brine of other people's tears."[13]

How original were Edwards's aphorisms? An examination of the standard books of quotations does not reveal any body of sources which appear to have given him a ready-made pool of raw materials. Yet Edwards may have been referring to himself in 1915 when he commented that "originality is merely a new way of expressing an old thought."[14] With his exposure in Scottish schools to the classics, as well as "dreary lectures" on moral philosophy, logic and metaphysics, Edwards was undoubtedly aware of the maxims of such philosophers as Socrates, Publilius Syrus, and Pliny the Elder.

For example, in 550 B.C. Aesop said, "We would often be sorry if our wishes were gratified,"[15] while in 1912, Bob Edwards commented, "There are times when we should be thankful for what we fail to get."[16]

Similarly, Pliny the Elder said, "It has become quite a common proverb that in wine there is truth,"[17] while Edwards observed, "A man when he's drunk will tell you all he knows —but what's the use?"[18] In the same vein, in the seventeenth century François, Duc de la Rochefoucauld, said, "We hardly find any persons of good sense save those who agree with us."[19] In turn, Bob Edwards said, "Isn't it queer that only sensible people agree with you?"[20]

In some cases, Edwards found a dozen different ways of expressing the same thought. For example, he believed that a man could easily turn against a friend and become an enemy. This maxim appeared in varying forms but always adhered to the same theme. He also found several ways to stereotype the jolliness of fat people, the inherent distrust women have for each other, and the basic dishonesty of man. While none of the themes may have been original with Edwards, he found unique ways of expressing them. In most cases, they also reflected his own cynicism towards life.

His "social notes," on the other hand, reveal a fascinating blend of fact, fiction and sexual suggestiveness which made the items one of his most popular features. Like the aphorisms, they first appeared in a regular way after Edwards returned to Calgary in 1912, probably starting simply as a means of poking fun at the pomposity of the social columns in the daily newspapers.

For example, in lampooning the practise by the social set of announcing the days when they would receive callers, Edwards wrote, "Mrs. Alex. P. Muggsy will not receive Friday. Mrs. Muggsy is insistent on this. She won't receive Friday under any consideration. If anybody comes around Friday they will get chucked out. Kindly therefore note that Mrs. Muggsy will not receive Friday. Better stay away Friday. Try Saturday."[21]

Similarly, poking fun at newspaper reports of social functions, he wrote, "A charming souse was held last Sunday at the bungalow of Mr. James T. Runion, the well known leader of the bachelor set. The affair was quite informal."[22]

In the beginning, the "social notes" were entirely fictitious, even to the names of the characters. However, as the years passed, Edwards found the items to be a convenient way of focussing attention on social or political issues. He slipped into the habit of sometimes using real names in fictitious circumstances, or fictitious names in describing actual events. In some instances, he also used a fully legitimate social note among the fictional ones.

When the police began to clamp down on dressmaking establishments which they believed were houses of prostitution, Edwards carried the following fictional note about a couple of well known *demi-mondes:* "Diamond Dolly has gone on a visit to the coast, leaving Miss Leta Long in full charge of her elegant dressmaking parlors."[23] On another occasion he wrote, "Miss Maude de Vere, of Drumheller, arrived in the city Wednesday and was run out of town the same night. It is a pity that Miss de Vere is not a racehorse, for she is very fast."[24]

The columns were a constant source of bewilderment and delight to readers of the *Eye Opener.* Which characters were real and which were fictional? Did those events really happen? So skillful was the blending of fact and imagination that Edwards's followers—particularly those outside Calgary—could never be certain.

Here are a number of the variations which often confronted and confounded the reader.

The first is entirely fictional. "Mrs. McSnuffy, who fell down the cellar steps and broke her neck at her charming residence on Mount Royal, will be greatly missed in booze-fighting circles. Her bottle was always open to her friends. O Rest in the Lord."[25]

The next combines a real person with a fictional event. "Hon. Crothers, Minister of Labor, has accepted an alluring offer to go into vaudeville, and will appear at Pantages very shortly in monologue. His contract called for a 15-minute humorous talk on his administration of the Labor department. It should elicit considerable laughter."[26]

The third note is entirely legitimate. "Premier Stewart was registered at the Palliser last week. He was driven round the city in the Sight Seeing Car and declared we had quite a burg here. This should be good for a few votes."[27]

And finally, this one likely deals with a real event, but uses fictional names. "The many friends of Peter F. Scratchley, the popular oil broker, will be glad to learn that he is rapidly recovering from a severe cold contracted while making a somewhat hasty departure, via the window, from the elegant mansion of the charming society matron, Mrs. J. T. Blinkbonny, at an early hour last Sunday morning."[28]

The introduction of prohibition in 1916 gave Edwards a perfect topic for his "social notes" and until his death in 1922, he liberally sprinkled his columns with booze parties, obituaries which mentioned that the widow had inherited a stock of liquor, and raids and arrests by the police. Other "social notes" dealt with such specialized topics as local elections, a visit of the Prince of Wales, and a Rotary Club convention.

These "social notes," like the aphorisms, had a role to play which went beyond simple humour. Besides ridiculing the social elite, the notes became another tool to attack the inequities and duplicities of Canadian society as Edwards saw them. At times, too, they became a means of ridiculing an individual in a humorous, deadly way. In matters of local politics, they also became vehicles for supporting a mayoralty or aldermanic candidate. Like other forms of Edwards's humour, the primary intent of the "social notes" was anything but funny.

The third group, Bob Edwards's jokes, were in a slightly different category. While some of them may have been original, many probably were adapted from British and American newspapers, sporting magazines and other publications to which Edwards subscribed. On a number of occasions he credited the sources, but for the most part, the reader was left to guess whether or not they originated with the Calgary editor. Many of them certainly reflected his writing style, and there can be little doubt that most of them received his special touch, even if only in editing.

Edwards showed a fondness for ethnic humour, particularly those in Scottish, Irish and German dialects. Over the years, his jokes also became more and more risque, so that charges of smuttiness and immorality levelled against the *Eye Opener* often were directed more towards the off-colour stories than his regular columns. The *Summer Annuals,* in particular, owed much of their success to the ribald jokes.

This was the role which Edwards had carefully and deliberately selected for his jokes. They were the means of gaining the readership of those who were not interested in politics or social issues. Like his sports stories, they aimed for those who would normally have avoided an ordinary political journal. The entertainment value of his jokes ensured the financial success of the *Eye Opener* through street sales, while at the same time building its reputation as a sensational sheet which was not afraid to print what it wanted. Of course, once a man had paid his nickel, there was a good chance he would also read Edwards's comments on the issues of the day.

As can be seen, the aphorisms, "social notes," and jokes were not simply random or accidental features of the *Eye Opener.* The editor was a brilliant and astute man who found a delicate balance between slashing editorials, philosophical cynicism, and his own brand of humour. Together, they created a newspaper which had the serious goal of attacking and, if possible, changing the social and political structure of Canada.

In spite of their purpose, however, many of the jokes are funny, the "social notes" ludicrous and the aphorisms filled with important truths which are as pertinent today as they were when written by Edwards more than half a century ago.

HUGH A. DEMPSEY

13

ACCURACY

The man who is always right is always a nuisance.

ADVERSITY

Sooner or later every man bumps into his stone wall.

Prosperity never spoils a man that adversity cannot crush.

ADVICE

If you are afflicted with a desire to give advice at every opportunity, become a lawyer or a doctor and sell it.

AGE

Anyway, the sign of old age is never a forgery.

Most people who are old enough to know better often wish they were young enough not to.

A woman begins to show her age only when she tries to hide it.

As a man grows older he sees something in himself every day that is calculated to make him a little less conceited.

The good don't die young at all. They simply outgrow it.

After one crosses the "roaring forties" of one's years one's notions of real excitement is a general election.

The experience of age is responsible for more mistakes than the inexperience of youth.

The other day Adam approached Peter at the pearly gates and said: "I should very much like, Peter, to get a pass to revisit my old haunts on earth."

"Nothing doing, Adam. You started too much trouble down there when you were a young man."

"Aw, Pete, be a good sport and let me go."

"What do you want to go down there for, anyhow?"

"I want to turn over another leaf."

Society Note— Mlle. Flossie Golightly, the charming booze artist, will have a tent on the Midway and give demonstrations of gulping down huge snorts of villainous whiskey without a chaser. Admission 25 cents. Miss Golightly was formerly a well-known fire-eater and sword swallower with Sir John Forbes Robertson's Shakespearean Company, on their tour through Canada some years ago. She will wear pink tights and throw in a few comic songs.

AMBITION

You will never get ahead by following the crowd.

It's all right to pray for the things you want, but it's a good idea to work for the things you need.

Most men are ambitious to do those they have been done by.

On these fine spring mornings the sun sets a good example by getting up as soon as it is daylight.

Hope for the best and then hustle for it.

Perhaps all things come to him who waits, but, considering the number of things not worth waiting for, a man is justified in going after what he wants.

A little push will generally last longer than a political pull. (Hear, hear!)

No man ever does as much today as he is going to do tomorrow.

Canadians want to be good friends with the Americans, but not to be a good square meal for them.

Say, you jolly Canucks, how do you like the prospect of becoming hewers of pulpwood and drawers of waterpower for the Americans?

An American sailor who had taken part in the war had taken the pains to have quite a bit of tattooing done on his body. After the war was over his ship had been ordered to Southern waters. While anchored down there some of the sailors went swimming. Amongst the lot was our hero.

They had been swimming around for some time, and unobserved by them was a shark sizing them up to decide which one would make a good lunch. He finally decided on our tattooed friend and was getting in position to bite when his eyes happened to see the writing on the body. The shark looked more intently and made out a picture of an American eagle, with the legend neatly tattooed underneath: "We Won the War."

The old shark was amazed and finally dived under. As he was going down, he was heard to mutter:
"My God! I can't swallow that."

A bull feeding in a field ate a buttercup containing a bee. While the bee was in the bull's mouth it thought of stinging it, but decided to wait until it was in its stomach. Arriving there, it fell asleep with the warmth.
Upon awakening, the bull was gone.

19

Don't get into the habit of going around with your bristles up.

How a man loves to find the house full of company when he comes home with something on his mind that he wants to scold about.

Beware of the man who grins when he gets angry.

Society Note— Mrs. Thos. F. Crawley gave an afternoon tea to a number of her friends last Tuesday at her residence in the West end. It really was tea that she served, and the guests left feeling very much disgusted, declaring that they would "lay off" the Crawleys in future.

APPLAUSE

Applause has made a fool of more men than criticism.

APPRECIATION

When anyone has done you a favor, how small it looks the day after.

Most people have good memories—except in regard to the favors done them.

ARGUMENT

When a man and a woman argue, the woman always gets the last word, but when two women argue the referee has to declare it a draw.

Be sure you're right—but don't be too sure that everybody else is wrong.

The repartee you think of when too late to work off, may save you a friend.

About the slowest way to settle an argument is to get two women interested in it.

Never judge an argument by its sound. It may be all sound or no sound at all.

Society Note— The debating society of the Y.M.C.A. held their usually weekly discussion last Wednesday evening in the basement of the Methodist church. The subject, "Is Square Gin or Old Tom the more Potent in a Collins?" led to rather an acrimonious debate, necessitating the calling in Mr. Tom Peers to give a final decision. The expert recommended a series of experiments and the following morning the city was in an uproar. This sort of thing is giving Calgary a bad name.

An Irishman came ambling into a hotel lobby, and shuffling up to the desk, leaned his elbows upon the cold stony counter, and slowly said to the clerk, "I want a room."

"Yes, sir. What kind?" asked the clerk.

"I want room 39."

"That's taken. I can give you another just as good."

"Don't want no other. I want Room 39."

"Sorry, sir, that room is now occupied. Here is Room 40 I know you will like it. James, show the gentleman to No. 40."

"I don't want it. I want Room 39."

"My dear sir," pleaded the patient clerk, "Room 39 is now occupied by Mr. Dennis M'Carthy."

"That's me. I have just fallen out of the window."

AUTOMOBILES

When Solomon said there was a time and a place for everything he had not encountered the problem of parking his automobile.

Occasionally a man has money in the bank because he doesn't own an automobile.

Society Note— The Bon Ton Literary Society held their first meeting of the season last Friday evening, the subject up for discussion being "Did Shakespeare or Bacon found the Winnipeg Free Press?" The question was decided in favor of Bacon, on the ground that the paper was on the hog.

BACHELORS

Bachelors are men who have illusions about women.

If a man is crazy and doesn't know it, it is because he has no wife to tell him.

Love is the wine of life and old bachelors are prohibitionists. What, ho!

There would be fewer old bachelors if single men were not allowed to associate with married men.

"Will you be my wife?" he asked.
"No," she replied. So he remained a bachelor and lived happily ever after.

BANKRUPTCY

Bankruptcy is when you put your money in your hip pocket and let your creditors take your coat.

BAR-ROOM

One trouble with the bar-room as a "poor man's club" is that the annual dues are considerably higher than those of the rich man's club.

BEAUTY

Nearly every pretty girl can play the piano and nearly every homely girl is a good cook.

If a woman only knew how she looks when running to catch a car, she wouldn't.

If a girl has a pretty face, no man on earth can tell you what kind of clothes she has on.

Fortunately for his peace of mind, the average man is unable to realize how homely he is.

Society Note— Miss Mamie Taylor has accepted a position as typewriter and stenographer in the law office of Quirk, Gammon and Snap, a well-known Toronto firm of shysters. Miss Taylor will be much missed by her numerous friends here, though it is not likely she will cut much tobacco with the Toronto gallants owing to her being about as pretty as a brickyard.

BLUFF

The proof of the bluffer is his failure to make good.

Bluff is often a good substitute for brains.

One "made good" is better than a dozen bluffs.

BOASTFULNESS

One good thing about a dog fight is that the dogs engaged in it do not go around and talk for publication after it is all over.

When a woman talks nothing but small talk, she is almost as bad as the man who always talks big.

Several ladies sat after a card party a few mornings ago discussing the virtues of their husbands.
"Mr. Bingleton," said one of them, referring to her life partner, "never drinks and never swears—indeed he has no habits."
"Does he ever smoke?" someone asked.

"Yes; he likes a cigar just after he has eaten a good meal. But, I suppose on an average he doesn't smoke more than once a month."

BOOZE

The ability to take a drink and let it alone takes constant practise.

You can learn more about a man by taking ten drinks with him than you can by going to church with him for ten years.

The cup that cheers is a noisy piece of crockery.

Before marrying a booze fighter to reform him, a girl should learn the gentle art of chasing soiled linen up and down a washboard.

Gallons of trouble can come out of a pint flask.

The dryness, or otherwise, of the coming summer depends largely on the bootleggers.

Some men are hard drinkers, but others find it absurdly easy.

Confound these bootleggers! They ought to be shot. You can never find one when you want him!

We should be the last to crack jokes at the expense of the fair sex. We have sometimes been as badly frightened by an imaginary snake as any of the I.O.D.E.'s ever were by a real mouse.

Some men borrow trouble because they have heard that it drives men to drink.

Any man who drinks is sure to marry a woman with a delicate sense of smell. The female of the species is more dangerous than a whale.

Look not upon the wine when it is red. Drink gin.

The suggestion has been made that our talented bootleggers be sent to the North Pole, where they will have less latitude.

The melancholy days have come,
   the saddest of the year;
It's a little too warm for whiskey,
   and a little too cold for beer.

Society Note— The raid of Mrs. Frances Trollop's delightful residence in Elbow Park by the provincial police last Tuesday night was void of results. No liquor of any kind was found on the premises. They evidently overlooked examining Mrs. Trollop's charming flowerpots on the veranda. We had a charming jolt out of one of them last week.

But hark! What do we hear? Footsteps coming down the hall—pause outside the door—a knock. It is the laddie with the bottle. Wasn't long, was he? Ah, where is that corkscrew? —Oh, here it is in its accustomed place. Good old corkscrew. Well, you'll have to excuse us for a minute.

Society Note— Miss Lottie McGlory, the debonair blond sport who took the part of Nell Gwynne, Charles the Second's extra-special, on the main float in the H.B.C. *parade, was entertained at a blow-out Wednesday night by the Sons of Bonnie Scotland. Miss McGlory, who is known amongst her friends as "the Arid Belt," because she is always dry, certainly cleaned up on the booze on this occasion.*

The Boozery:
The hours I spent with thee, dear heart,
   Are memories dear to me;
For years I poured thee o'er and o'er,
   My Johnnie Dewar, my Johnnie Dewar!

CEREMONY

Ceremony was invented by a wise man to keep fools at a distance.

CHILDREN

The world will never get any better until children are an improvement on their parents.

One reason why fewer children are tied to their mother's apron strings nowadays is that fewer mothers wear aprons.

A woman never stops to consider how very uninteresting her children would be if they were some other woman's.

CIVILIZATION

We wonder what the sky will look like when the world celebrates the one hundredth anniversary of aviation.

One of the pleasures of living in this age is to watch the things being done that a little while ago most people said could not be done.

The future is what the past might have been, but wasn't.

No matter how early one gets up, somebody is just coming home, and no matter how late one stays up, somebody is just going to work. A city is the apothesis of the absurdity of civilization.

If the Almighty had allowed the conquerors of ancient times to fool with high explosives, submarines and such like, there would have been no posterity, meaning us.

This is a swift age. If your name is in the list of "also rans" you are doing fairly well.

We believe that modern warfare is doomed. It is unthinkable that the civilized world of the future will permit this coldly scientific and impersonal method of settling differences among nations to survive. Its infamy is too apparent.

"Papa, the preacher was here to lunch today."
"You don't mean it."
"Yes; and he swore about mother's cooking the same as you do, only he put his hand over his eyes."

Another mistake the city of Calgary is making is in driving all the prostitutes from Nose Creek and scattering them throughout the city. Why not leave them where they were and allow them to attend to their own business in a businesslike way. It is impossible to put a stop to this traffic, so why scatter them into the decent part of the city?

CLEVERNESS

Occasionally a man is clever enough to know how important he isn't.

Sooner or later a wise fish runs across a bait that fools him.

CONCEIT

A conceited man is one who wants to talk about himself when you want to talk about yourself.

Every man thinks he is more important than his neighbor.

A man is never ridiculous for what he is, but for assuming to be what he isn't.

The man who takes himself seriously may be considered a joke by others.

A man could learn a great many things if he didn't imagine that he already knew them.

Don't get too self-important. The world will go on just the same after you get out.

Every man has an idea, or has had, that he is either clever or good-looking.

You can't reform a man by telling him that he ought to be as good as you are.

It always amuses a woman when she sees a man posing as a wise guy.

If a man is ignorant he may learn, but if he knows too much there is no hope for him.

Any man who knows it all must be an awful bore to himself.

He who thinks only of himself has very little to think about.

A red-haired woman has as much right to call her hair golden as a fat woman has to call herself plump.

The difference between a country youth and a city youth is that the former wants to know everything and the latter thinks he knows it all.

When we hear a man boasting about how awfully smart his wife is, we wonder if she was temporarily insane when she married him.

CONSCIENCE

Conscience is a watchdog that barks at sin.

A man may take on sufficient booze to disable his conscience temporarily, but it will be doing business at the old stand next morning.

When you feel like doing a foolish thing remember that you have to live with your memory.

It's easier for a real estate man to make money if he isn't on speaking terms with his conscience.

"They say that the cause of their quarrel was a letter his wife found in his pocket."
"One he had forgotten to mail?"
"No, one he had forgotten to burn."

We learn that Miss Mary E. Frobisher, of Didsbury, is engaged to be married to the well-known Calgarian, Mr. John

T. Billcoe, on Nov. 20. It is apparent that Titania was not the only woman who loved a donkey.

CONTENTMENT

Contentment consists largely in not wanting something that is out of your reach.

Be content, but never satisfied.

Any man who doesn't want what he hasn't got has all he wants.

A man can get along without doing much if he has sense enough to know what not to do.

Contentment may mean lack of desire.

CONTRARY-MINDEDNESS

Among contrary men is the chap who would refuse to take whiskey if the doctor prescribed it.

More people would go to church if it wasn't exactly the proper thing to do.

A Macleod jury recently brought in the following verdict: "We find the prisoner guilty as charged, but we do not believe he is the right man."

COURAGE

He who loses money loses a little; he who loses a friend loses more, and he who loses courage loses most.

If your luck isn't what it should be, write a 'p' in front of it and try again.

"Who was the bravest man you ever met, colonel?"
"Phil Miggs, they called him."
"And what was his most courageous act?"

"He married a widow whose first three husbands had each committed suicide."

CREDIT

Don't boast of your credit. No man's credit is as good as his money.

It is always the man who can get credit for the asking who doesn't want it.

If your credit isn't good you can easily cut down expenses.

Lack of credit prevents some people from living beyond their means.

A preferred creditor is one who never troubles you.

A man's credit is seldom good if he is unable to make good.

"Mary," said the sick man to his wife, after the doctor had pronounced it a case of smallpox, "if any of my creditors call, tell them that I am in a position to give them something."

CRITICISM

The badness in the best of us and the goodness in the worst of us should restrain any of us from throwing mud at the rest of us.

It is surprising how many things a man can find to criticize and how few he will commend.

If you want honest criticism of anything you do, tell your friends that it is the work of another, and then they will be free to give their opinion that the man who did it was bughouse.

Society Note— Miss Jessie Marshfield is staying in Banff for a few days, nursing her alleged father, whose addiction to whiskey is most distressing to his friends, especially as he seldom has the price.

If the public bites, the bark of the critic is harmless.

Don't judge yourself too harshly. You can depend on others doing that.

CURIOSITY

The less a man says the more guessing his wife has to do.

Why have so many people that faculty of finding out things that are none of their business?

Men are said to be quite as much afflicted with curiosity as women are supposed to be. We can well believe this.

There are two reasons why some people do not mind their own business: one is because they haven't any business, the other is because they haven't any mind.

Women wonder why a man is always hitching up his trousers when he wears a belt. Curiosity is woman's besetting sin.

Snoozer: "What star were you born under?"
Boozer: "Three-Star Hennessy."

CYNICISM

Cynicism is merely the art of seeing things as they are, instead of as they ought to be.

Society Note— Mayor Brown, of Medicine Hat, is to attend the Industrial Research Conference next week in Edmonton. He will find that the only research that interests them up there is whiskey. When they don't find it the first time, they research.

Society Note— Mrs. Jonathan Wilder gave an at home Thursday to a few friends whose aid she was enlisting on behalf of her husband, who is out as a candidate in the municipal elections. There was no booze and the function was a miserable frost. Mr. Wilder has no more chance than a snowball in hell.

"I'll never forget the night you proposed," said his wife. "You acted like a fish out of water."
"Yes, I was a sucker."

DEATH

Life is bottled sunshine. Death the silent-footed butler who removes the cork. Pop!

After a man has one foot in the grave it doesn't take him long to get there with both feet.

This is a dry world. Those of us who eventually wind up in hell should burn brightly.

Just about the time a man gets comfortably fixed in this world it is time for him to move on to the next.

Trying to find the good in everything, one is delighted to learn that the modern bullet is more sanitary than the old. This should be a great comfort to the slain.

At the resurrection there will be mighty few come to the surface in some of our Western cemeteries. About two-thirds will drop through the other way.

Society Note— The many friends of T. B. Sweeney, of the North Hill, will be delighted to hear that he accidently blew the top of his head off with a shotgun last Wednesday, while crawling through a fence on a duck-hunting trip. Mr. Sweeney was a miserable specimen and his demise is the cause of much rejoicing in the neighborhood. Mrs. Sweeney celebrated the occasion by hitting up Kennedy's Tonic Bitters, her yells being distinctly heard on this side of the river.

Said the father impressively to his irrevent son: "Suppose I should be taken away suddenly, what would become of you?"

"I'd stay here. The question is, what would become of you?"

Society Note— Death with his sickle keen never pulled a more popular stunt than when he picked off old Daniel Warrenton, of Crescent Heights, last week. Deceased had become a veritable nuisance and it was only a question of time when he would have been murdered.

DIGNITY

Although a dignified man may not know much, he has to be very careful of what little he does know.

DILLUSION

If dillusions would make a man happy what a jolly old world this would be.

DIPLOMACY

People sometimes stir up a lot of trouble by telling the truth when it would be policy to say nothing.

Praise men and flatter women and you will have many fair weather friends.

Every boy should learn to write, and if he ever becomes an editor he should learn what not to write.

A polite person is one who doesn't let other people know what he thinks of them.

With a little diplomacy any woman can induce her husband to buy her a new hat. All she has to do is to visit his office, arrayed in one of her own make.

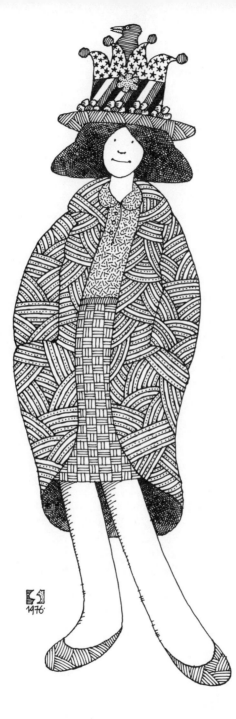

If a diplomat says "Yes," he may mean "Maybe";
If he says "Maybe," he means "No";
If he says "No," he is no diplomat.

If a lady says "No," she may mean "Maybe";
If she says "Maybe," she means "Yes";
If she says "Yes," she is no lady.

He was a collector for an installment system establishment, new at the business, and very sensitive about performing his unpleasant task. He was particularly embarrassed because the lady upon whom he had called was so exceedingly polite and beautiful. Still, the van was at the door, the lady was in arrears in her payments, and he remembered his duty.

"Good morning," said the lady. "It is a beautiful day, is it not? Won't you take a chair?"

"Er — No, thank you, not this morning," he stammered. "I think I'll take the piano."

Society Note— Hank Borden, who was hanged at Lethbridge last week for a most atrocious murder, is no relation to Sir Robert Borden, premier of Canada. Sir Robert expects the present session to be a short one.

DISCOURAGEMENT

When you are discouraged and think there is no use trying, then get busy.

The darkest hour is when you haven't a match.

Society Note— The bridge party which was to have been given by Mrs. Peter McSnuffy at her charming residence on Mount Royal last Wednesday had to be called off at the last minute. The whiskey laid in for the occasion had inadvertently been lapped up by McSnuffy the previous evening.

DISHONESTY

Few men appear to be as bad as they really are.

A good man who goes wrong is just a bad man who has been found out.

Every man does things on the quiet that would make him feel quite small if they were found out.

Some men are so constructed that they simply have to swindle somebody, and rather than be idle they will bunco their friends. Any one who resided in Calgary for any length of time will endorse this observation.

Crooked ways often lead to straightened circumstances.

Many a man, naturally honest, goes lame when an opportunity worth while knocks at his door.

The average man shows up all right on the surface, but few can stand probing.

There is a great deal printed that you can't believe— especially on bottles.

"Will you please furnish me with a description of your missing cashier?" asked the detective. "For instance, how tall is he?"
"I don't know how tall he was," replied the boss, testily. "What worries me is that he was $50,000 short."

Society Note— Mr. and Mrs. Alex Hamden, of Fourteenth Ave. W., entertained a party of friends for Thanksgiving dinner last Monday. At the close of the repast the genial host returned a thanks to the Almighty for the blessing vouchsafed him that he was not in jail, some surprise having been expressed in various quarters that he was at large.

"You have a pretty tough looking lot of customers to dispose of this morning, haven't you?" remarked a friend of the magistrate.
"Huh!" rejoined the dispenser of justice. "You are looking at the wrong bunch. Those are the lawyers."

DISSATISFACTION

You are like all the rest, we suppose? Dissatisfied with what you have and what you haven't.

If a man and his job are not congenial, little is accomplished.

It is easy to be content with what we have—it's what we haven't that worries us.

One always thinks there is a lot of money to be made in any kind of business he isn't in.

DOCTORS

Every doctor in a small town is fully convinced that he would have become world famous had he located in a city.

"Heart failure" covers a lot of medical ignorance.

"I hope you are following the instructions carefully, Sandy —the pills three times a day and a drop of whiskey at bedtime."
"Weel, sir, I may be a wee bit behind wi' the pills, but I'm about six weeks in front wi' the whusky."

DOUBTS

"If" is the most unsatisfactory word in our language, and "but" comes next.

"Why did you leave your last place?"
Mary Anne—"Well, mum, when a bullock died we got beef till it finished. When a sheep died we got mutton till it was finished, and when the cat died—I left."

Society Note— Mrs. McSnuffy, who fell down the cellar steps and broke her neck at her charming residence on Mount Royal, will be greatly missed in booze-fighting circles. Her bottle was always open to her friends. O Rest in the Lord.

Drug addiction is a natural consequence of prohibition. A drinker of whiskey is sure to find a substitute if it be within his or her reach when whiskey is beyond it.

DRUNKENNESS

Gallons of trouble come out of a pint flask.

No doubt about it all. The first drink is the Adam of a drunk.

There are a great many things that drive a man to drink, but the principal one is thirst.

He's the meanest kind of man who will rob his own family to pay for another man's drink.

A man when he's drunk will tell you all he knows—but what's the use?

When the busy little bee gets a load he goes straight home —which is more than a man can do.

Women have queer ideas of a good time, but they seldom have a dark brown taste next morning.

Getting drunk is likely to become much more of a luxury than ever—if it ever was a luxury.

You may be justified in blowing your own horn, but not in going on a toot.

Next time you're drunk, try and say: "She stood at the gate welcoming him in." Bet you can't do it.

Some men take a drink naturally and some others are quite willing to be taken.

Society Note— Mr. Peter T. Ferguson, a highly respected drunk from Lethbridge, spent a couple of days in the city last week. He expressed surprise at the growth of the city.

"Thash all right, m'dear, thashallright. Not my fault thish-time. Been tempransh lecshur and drank in every word. Man mush said whiskey thousand times, shoushan' times."

"Society Note— The many friends of Mrs. Frederick P. Sloshencruncher will be delighted to learn that her husband is now convalescent and rapidly recovering from his recent attack of delirium tremens. Mrs. Sloshencruncher will resume her delightful afternoon musicales this summer.

DUPLICITY

What's the use of trying to fool a man who has no money?

There comes a time in the life of almost every married man when he says, "What my wife doesn't know won't hurt her."

When a man offers you something for nothing, don't accept it unless you can afford to pay double what it is worth.

A young man may fool a girl as to what wages he gets, but he can't fool her father.

It's easier for a woman to fool any man than it is to keep him fooled.

Some people are always up and doing—other people.

Ever notice that no politician ever poses as a reformer while in office.

It's easy for a woman to fool a man who thinks he can't be fooled. What?

A Scotchman came upon an automobile overturned at a railway crossing. Beside it lay a man all smashed up.
"Get a doctor," he moaned.
"Did the train hit you?" asked the Scotchman.
"Yes, yes, get a doctor."
"Has the claim agent been here yet?"
"No, no; please get a doctor."
"Move over, you," said the Scot, "till I lie down beside you."

Society Note— The wedding of Miss Carolina Kopp, of Sunnyside, and Mr. George L. Blooey, of the North Hill, was declared off at the last moment when old man Kopp discovered that Mr. Blooey had a wife and five children living in England and another spouse in the States somewhere. Mr. Blooey enjoyed the joke as much as anybody and laughed heartily at the absurd contretemps.

A man was astonished to receive the following letter from his son in the city:

"Dear father: I am in a deuce of a hole. Kindly send me $50 and oblige. Your loving son, Pat.

"P.S.—After writing this letter I was so stricken with remorse that I ran after the postman and tried to get it back. I can only pray that it will not reach you."

But who could be more astounded than the son when he received this reply:

"Dear Son: Your prayers are answered. The letter did not reach me. Father."

ECONOMY

A woman's idea of economy is to have things charged.

EFFICIENCY

A hard worker may not be the best worker.

It takes a woman who doesn't know how to do a thing to do it better than a man who knows all about it.

ELOQUENCE

Eloquence is ordinary gab with its Sunday clothes on.

ENEMIES

A man's most bitter enemy is the friend who can no longer work him.

The editor of this rag is beginning to be loved for the enemies he has fooled.

A man may not know who his friends are but he usually has his enemies spotted.

Most of a man's friends are ready to become his enemies on the least provocation.

A man who has no enemies is seldom good for anything. We derive much comfort from this reflection.

The loss of a friend adds one to the list of your enemies.

Society Note— The Calgary Eye Opener's *Radio Scotch Concert will be given as soon as Mr. Macpherson, our broadcaster, sobers up. Mr. Macpherson is the most drunken broadcaster in the business. No doubt about it.*

ENVY

Some folks try to get up in the world by throwing stones at men who have reached the top.

EVIL

If you play with the devil, you lose.

EXPECTATIONS

Blessed are they who expect little, for they usually get it.

If you expect nothing, then whatever you do get is velvet.

FAILURE

Only the man who is a failure sneers at success.

The man who has never tried has no sympathy for the one who has tried and failed.

Some men are known by the company they are unable to get into.

FAITH

Faith is a belief in something you know isn't so.

The less faith other people have in a man, the more his wife has.

They were talking about their friends.
"And what do you think of Jones?"
"I'd trust him with my life."
"Yes, I know. But would you trust him with five dollars?"
"Oh, no."

FAME

All the world's a stage, but few of us get in the spotlight.

Many a great and important man—that is, great and important in the eyes of others—is but a wart on a pickle in the eyes of his wife.

There are lots of great men until you get close to them.

Any man who itches for fame will have to do a lot of scratching before he gets there.

No man is a nonentity unless he is the husband of a too prominent woman.

The more reputation a man has, the more disappointed other men are when they meet him.

FASHION

If there were no such thing as fashion, half the workmen in the world would lose their jobs.

As winter begins to display its large supply of weather, men begin to wonder why more women do not have pneumonia.

Of course it takes nerve on a girl's part to wear extremely short skirts, but there are a couple of other reasons too.

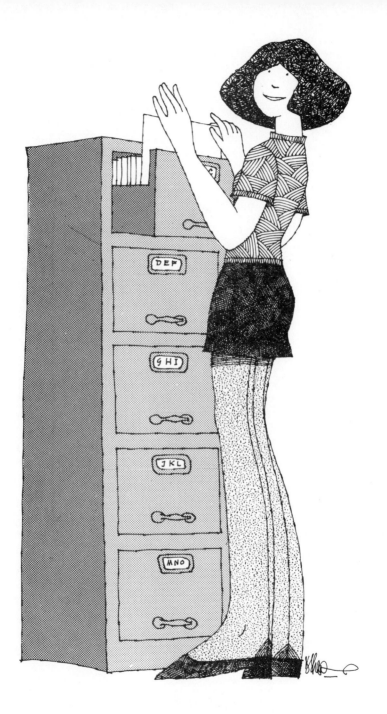

One form of innocence consists in wondering how it happens that the girl with the prettiest ankles wears the shortest skirt.

It is the things that are made to look at that cost the most.

For the correct meaning of "low visibility" just cast your lamps on the first girl you meet coming down the street in short skirts.

A girl recently informed her mother that she didn't intend to wear short skirts any longer.

What has become of the old-fashioned female of the species who never wore any kind of shoes except black?

A lovely woman on a windy day resembles nothing so much as a parachute that has just made a successful landing.

Etiquette— If on entering a drawing room full of ladies you trip on a rug and fall headlong in amongst them, do not make matters worse by assuring them that you have been on the water wagon for three months. This kind of apology is in execrable taste and they don't believe you anyhow.

It must be awfully discouraging to the health fans to find that despite their tight shoes, short skirts, corsets, collarless gowns and foolish little hats, women continue to grow prettier and healthier. Whereas careful men grow grey and wheezy and bald-headed and bottlenosed and ridiculous in every way.

Society Note— Miss Lottie McSquawker entertained informally at her charming home on Fifth Ave. East, Wednesday night. She cheerfully paid her fine Thursday morning and left the police station looking quite chic in her imitation Hudson seal.

FLATTERY

If a man tells a woman she is beautiful she will overlook most of his other lies.

When an opportunity occurs for kind words, deliver the goods.

If you want to hear a woman cackle, tell her she looks chic.

The wise man follows the line of least resistance when he tells the mother how beautiful her kid is.

If a man tells a woman she has a musical laugh she will fall for any old joke he may get off.

FOOLISHNESS

It is a waste of life to be sensible all the time.

It's easy to be happy. All you have to do is to be foolish.

It is part of human nature to think wise things and do ridiculous ones.

No man can make a fool of himself all of the time. He has to sleep occasionally.

It is almost as easy to achieve foolishness as it is to be born foolish.

It's an easy matter to furnish entertainment for your neighbors; all you have to do is make a fool of yourself.

Oh, well, when we think of all the fool things we didn't do that we might have done (and wanted to do at the time), we almost forgive ourselves for the uncountable damfool things we have done.

Many a sensible man seems dull because he lacks a little foolishness.

Any man who can't remember when he was a fool is one yet.

Society Note— Mr. J. M. Buchanan, of Twelfth Ave. West, was arrested last Tuesday for having fourteen cases of Scotch whiskey in his house. He explained to the bench that he was

preparing to run in East Calgary against M. C. Costello,
whereupon the magistrate made out the papers for his removal
to Ponoka. Mr. Buchanan has been practising law in the city.

A policeman, whose evidence was being taken on com-
mission, deposed:
"The prisoner sat upon me, calling me an ass, a scarecrow,
a ragamuffin, and an idiot," and, this being the conclusion of
his depositions, his signature was preceded by the formal end-
ing: "All of which I swear is true."

FRIENDSHIP

Better a fool friend than a wise enemy.

No, that's right. A man's friends seldom work overtime on
the friendship job.

If a man never has anybody to tell him what he would do
in his place, he is friendless.

When a man is down his enemies stop kicking him and
his friends begin.

Set 'em up and the crowd is with you. Go broke and you
go it alone.

The difference between a friend and an acquaintance is
that a friend helps where an acquaintance merely advises.

Only true friends stand by you when you are under a
cloud. Swarms of insects surround you when the sun shines.

And it frequently comes to pass that by helping our friends
they become our enemies, and by helping our enemies they
become our friends.

He is truly a great man who can lose his money and still
retain his friends.

The average man has more friends and fewer enemies than
he thinks he has.

One way to break a friendship is to go broke yourself.

A friend will always laugh at your jokes, be they good or bad, but there's a great deal in the way he does it.

You can always depend upon the enmity of your enemies, but there are times when you cannot depend upon the friendship of your friends.

If a man is always making new friends it is a sign that his old friends are onto him.

The worst thing about friends is the ease with which they are converted into enemies.

Our idea of a misguided man is one who thinks his friends are as glad to have him visit them as he thinks they are.

The bottom soon drops out of quickly-made friendship.

A man in trouble always appreciates a friend — until he gets out of it.

A true friend is one who listens to your hard-luck story.

"You have a great many friends."
"I don't know so much about that. I've never been broke."

FRUSTRATION

The clock invariably strikes the half-hour when you wake up in the night and you want to know what time it is.

A mean man is one who will deliberately say things in his sleep for the purpose of keeping his tired wife awake.

Society Note— There was only one case of sleeping sickness in Calgary last week. No alarm was felt by the medical health officer, as the patient, W. T. Ruggles, always takes about three days to sleep off a drunk. He was up and about yesterday, looking quite spry.

54

FUSSINESS

A fussy man gets in his own way when he is in a hurry.

With the exception of a fussy woman, there is nothing on earth so disagreeable as a fussy man.

FUTURE

Did it ever occur to you that now is the future you longed for several years ago?

GAMBLING

Success at poker depends on the way a man is raised.

Many a would-be poker player makes a mistake in his calling.

When a man tells you what a wonderful poker player you are, that man is planning to enjoy life at your expense.

Authorities differ as to whether a poker room should be classed as an ante-room or a drawing room.

GENEROSITY

The man who would give his last dollar seldom possesses a nickel.

GLUTTONY

Anyway, a fat woman seldom has a disagreeable temper.

If a woman is thin she can fix it some way, but there is no hope for the fat ones.

Fat men are good natured because good natured men are usually fat.

"It's hard," said the sentimental landlady at the dinner table, "to think this poor little lamb should be destroyed in its youth, just to cater to our appetites."

"Yes," replied the smart boarder, struggling with his portion, "It is tough."

GOLF

If you must play golf on Sunday, play good golf.

Golf a rich man game? Nonsense! Look at all the poor players.

Did you ever notice how careful the Venus de Milo was not to have her statue carved in some ridiculous golfing posture?

"How is your husband getting on with his golf?"
"Very well, indeed. The children are allowed to watch him now."

GOODNESS

The goodness of people is exceedingly tiresome.

Why does a man who is really good usually look so sad?

After a man's goodness reaches a certain point, he begins to take a day off occasionally.

Any man who poses as a model citizen has a dam hard job.

No matter how bad a man may be, there is one woman who can find some good in him.

A feeling of superiority is the sole satisfaction some men get out of being good.

Many an earthly saint has a face that scares away temptation. (That's no lie. Ed. E.O.)

You may depend upon it that he is a good man whose intimate friends are all good, and whose enemies are decidedly bad.

It is well that there is no one without a fault, for he would not have a friend in the world.

No man particularly admires a woman who is so good that all her women acquaintances like her.

GOOD DEEDS

If you intend to do a mean thing, wait till tomorrow; but if you are going to do good, do it now.

GOSSIP

Be careful how you let remarks fall—they may hurt a friend.

A person who tells you the faults of others will tell others of yours.

A woman who says a mean thing about another woman isn't half as mean as the woman who repeats it.

This would be a better world if everybody would take a five-year holiday from gossip.

Gossips have no use for people who refuse to supply them with raw material.

Any man who repeats half what he hears talks too much.

Girls should remember that when they confide in a married woman they are probably confiding in her husband also.

A gossip has few friends, but she manages to get good and even with her numerous enemies.

Gossip is a vulgar habit, and other people should not indulge in it.

Whisper slander in confidence to your best friend, and though you stand on a hill the next day and proclaim in a loud voice that it is not true, you cannot call the bad story back.

If you would know what your friends say about you when you are absent, listen to what is said about others in your presence.

A good deal of conversation should be canned and the can thrown away.

Our idea of a trouble-maker is any citizen or citizeness with a nose for news and the gift of the gab.

A woman has as little use for a secret she can't tell as she has for money she can't spend.

We say just as mean things about others as they do about us, but of course that is different.

A lot of conversation worked off in society ought to be dumped in the garbage can.

Society Note— The many friends of Mrs. T. Tinglebuster, of Elbow Park, who recently underwent an operation for appendicitis, will be glad to learn that she is dead. She was an awful bore.

Society Note— James T. Blaney, prominent in Calgary real estate circles, died last Tuesday at his home on Fourth Ave. West. Nobody will miss Blaney. He was no good.

GRAFT

Perhaps a shorter definition of graft and one that would fit in the vocabulary of politicians is: "A good thing that you are not in on."

A clever politician is one who is able to cover up his tracks. Otherwise he is just a dam grafter.

GREED

Some men drop all their money trying to pick up more.

GUILE

It might be well to remember that every man you deal with is looking for the best of it.

The man who is able to feather his own nest this winter must be a bird.

Society Note— John F. Ballington, one of our most prominent and intelligent citizens, met with a nasty accident last Thursday night; while hastily climbing down the rain pipe from a lady's bedroom window, on one of our fashionable avenues, he lacerated his hand on a jagged piece of lead. The wounded member was dressed by his family physician and little danger is expected from blood-poisoning.

A man who had purchased a fine looking horse soon discovered that the animal was blind, and after several weeks he succeeded is disposing of her, as the defect did not seem to lessen her speed nor detract from her general appearance. The next day the new owner of the horse appeared.

"Say, you know that mare you sold me?" he began. "She's stone blind."

"I know it," replied her past owner with an easy air.

"You didn't say anything to me about it," said the purchaser, his face red with anger.

"Well, you see," replied the other, "the fellow who sold her to me didn't tell me about it and I just concluded that he didn't want it known."

GULLIBILITY

If there was not a sucker born every minute the other half of the world would starve to death.

The wise guy who knows it all is usually the first to get stung.

People always laugh at the fool things you try to do, until they discover you are making money out of them.

It is as hard to impose on some men the second time as it was easy to impose on them the first time.

"Young man, can you write real estate ads?"
"You bet I can, sir. I have published a volume of fairy tales and am author of a revised edition of the Arabian Nights."
"Well, consider yourself engaged. Get busy on Boozeness Park."

HAPPINESS

Tomorrow is the happiest day in a man's life.

Never sigh when you can sing.

Be agreeable and see how quickly things begin coming your way.

Be good and you'll be happy—perhaps.

There would be less trouble in this world if people were permitted to be happy in their own way.

The more bad habits a man has, the more he seems to enjoy life's good things.

The world deals goodnaturedly with a goodnatured person.

Happiness has a peculiar way of coming and going without any warning.

Happiness is the result of being poor and respectable— according to the storybooks.

An exclamation of joy comes 4th when a mother discovers her baby's 1st 2th.

At least it may be said for the industrious cockroach that it never whistles or sings as it goes about its duties in the kitchen.

What happy lives farmers live in storybooks! Strictly between ourselves, did you ever see a happy farmer?

Society Note— Mr. James Howell, the well-known professor of Arts and Sciences at Youngstown, dropped in to the Eye Opener office Wednesday and wished the staff a merry Xmas. He expressed himself as delighted at finding the staff, who is ourself, comparatively sober.

Society Note— John T. Freeney, of Red Deer, dropped down to Calgary last week on business. Being interdicted in his home town, Mr. Feeney derives much enjoyment in these trips abroad.

HIGHBROW

Oh, you want to know what a highbrow is, eh? Well, a highbrow is a person who has an habitual attitude of contempt toward that which is popular and also a person whose education is generally beyond his intelligence.

HISTORY

If it is all the same to history, it need not repeat itself any more.

History records the one race won by an easy-going tortoise, but never says a word about the many previous races won by the hare.

HOMES

Home is the place where many a man shows up at a disadvantage.

Homes should always be kept neat and clean, because company may walk in at any moment.

A man never quite realizes how much furniture he owns until he tries to walk rapidly through his rooms in the dark.

HONESTY

Nearly all men believe that honesty in moderation is the best policy.

What a man is when alone, is what he is.

It is believed by some credulous persons that the time—ha ha!—will come when an honest man will command respect. More ha-ha's.

There is one thing in the small boy's favor—he never pretends to like anybody he doesn't.

It is easy to convince a man that honesty is the best policy —if it pays better.

The way to gain a good reputation is to endeavor to be what you desire to appear. (Socrates said that.)

Don't place too much confidence in a man who boasts of being as honest as the day is long. Wait until you meet him at night.

Never accuse a man of being honest until you know the amount of money he has been offered to keep his face closed, to cast his vote against his conscience, or to advocate a wrong course of action.

Etiquette Note— When asking a lady if she would care for some refreshments it is considered a mark of ill-breeding to say, "How would a horn strike you?" or "What's the matter with a snifter?" Such cryptic terms presuppose too much familiarity with boozology on the part of the lady. It is much more comm-il-faut *to bow politely and say,* "*If you are feeling dry, Miss Fewclothes, I believe I could rustle you a snort.*"

"*Can you write shorthand?*"
"*Oh, yes; only it takes me a little longer.*"

A Scotch lassie was being examined by the minister, who said: "*Well, I trust ye hae never broken any o' the ten commandments?*"
"*No, sir,*" *she coyly replied,* "*but I hae chipped yen or twa.*"

HUMOR

An ounce of jolly goes farther than a ton of advice.

Sometimes the humor of a man is so dry that he has to buy drinks to get anybody to listen to it.

People are always trying to dodge the man who thinks he can tell a funny story.

The best jokes told about a man are those he never hears.

It is almost impossible to discourage the man who thinks he can tell a funny story. In fact, it can't be done.

There are a lot of funny things in this world—besides men and women.

Tell the average man a joke and he will say, "That reminds me." Then he'll get busy and you will have to listen, and it serves you right.

IGNORANCE

Knowing things that are not so is the worst kind of ignorance.

A certain amount of ignorance is necessary to the enjoyment of our existence.

Many a train of thought gathers no freight.

1976.

An educated fool is more foolish than an ignorant one.

It's what a woman doesn't know about a man that causes her to have a good opinion of him.

Some people might just as well be crazy for all the sense they have.

Some people never change their minds because they are like a man with only one shirt.

Why, cert'nly. The nicest people are always those we don't know anything about.

When a man proclaims in a loud voice that he is a gentleman it's a safe bet he isn't. Especially if he pronounces it "gen'leman."

When charged with being drunk and disorderly and asked what he had to say for himself, the prisoner gazed pensively at the magistrate, smoothed down a remnant of grey hair and said:

"Your honor, man's inhumanity to man makes countless thousands mourn. I'm not as debased as Swift, as profligate as Byron, as dissipated as Poe, as debauched as . . . ."

"That will do," thundered the magistrate. "Ten days! And officer, take a list of those names and run 'em in. They are as bad a lot as he is!"

"And what did you enjoy most in France?" he asked the lady on her return from the trip.

"Well, in the rural districts I greatly enjoyed listening to the pheasants at work in the fields singing the Mayonnaise."

ILLUSIONS

Illusions are the grand ideas we have about ourselves; dillusions are the silly ideas other people have about us.

Some favorite fiction:
"Yes, I Can Take a Drink or I Can Let it Alone."

"My Friends are Urging Me to Become a Candidate for the Council."

"No, I Wouldn't go Across the Street to See a Prize Fight."

"I'm Always Pleased to Have a Friend Tell Me of My Faults."

"When I'm Thirsty Give Me a Glass of Cold Water Every Time."

INDEPENDENCE

If you don't owe a dollar you can look any man in the eye and tell him to go to hell.

INFLATION

What is needed is a dollar that will go further and develop less speed.

By some peculiar shift of values it appears that prices have come down in all things except those that one urgently needs.

The price of this paper is one dollar a year. It ought to be five, but we knock off four for irregularity.

One sighs for the good old times when a man could ask for a nickel's worth of something without being looked upon as a mendicant.

An Edmonton friend writes:
"Talking of the high cost of living, the only thing that is coming down is the rain and even that soaks you."

INGENUITY

Improved machinery enables a man to accomplish almost as many things as a woman with a hairpin.

INSPIRATION

Why does the bright idea we think of just before going to sleep depart, never to return?

INTELLIGENCE

If you think the average woman is weaker minded than the average man, you are entitled to another think.

After a long day's shooting some men were telling dog stories. Soon the tales got very tall, and a little man said:

"I have a dog that makes all yours seem fools. I generally feed him after dinner, but the other day a friend dropped in, and the poor beast slipped my mind. After the meal we went into the garden. The dog followed us, scratched up a flower, and put it at my feet with the most yearning look in his eyes. It was a forget-me-not!"

No more dog stories were told that evening.

JUDGMENT

Perhaps there is nothing quite as unsatisfactory as the good judgment a man might have used, but didn't.

KISSES

A girl's kisses are like pickles in a bottle—the first are hard to get, but the rest come easy.

KNOWLEDGE

If you want to become intelligent you must take your own little pitcher to the well of knowledge and dip it in yourself.

Nearly all the knowledge in the world has been acquired at the expense of somebody's burnt fingers.

The day has passed when one can pretend to know things. People want to be shown.

He knows most who knows he doesn't know it all.

Nine-tenths of what the average man knows is of no earthly benefit to him.

LAUGHTER

The laughter and tears of a woman are equally deceptive.

Half the battle is won if you start the day with a laugh.

If we could neither laugh nor cry, life would not be worth living.

The public will pay more for laughing than for any other privilege.

There is no hope for the man who begrudges himself an occasional hearty laugh.

He who laughs best may be merely slow of comprehension.

Lots of grown folks are as hard to amuse as a baby.

"Want to go to the theatre tonight, wifie?"
"I have nothing to wear."
"Then we'll go to the movie where it's dark."

Society Note— Mrs. Alex P. Muggsy will not receive Friday. Mrs. Muggsy is insistent on this. She won't receive Friday under any consideration. If anybody comes around Friday they will get chucked out. Kindly therefore note that Mrs. Muggsy will not receive Friday. Better stay away Friday. Try Saturday.

LAZINESS

He who never does wrong never does much anyway.

72

Some men are too lazy to kick when they get the short end of it.

Lazy men bump against a lot of criticism, but they usually live long and contented lives.

Were it not for the lazy men in the world lots of labor-saving devices would never have been invented.

LEAP YEAR

A man is not supposed to do the proposing in a leap year. The best he can do is file a protest.

Even if a man did accept a leap year proposal, he would refuse to admit it.

LEISURE

Take a day or a week off occasionally, and your year will accumulate more slowly.

When a sociable man has a minute to spare he goes and bothers some man who is busy.

Some men never work harder than when they are doing useless things without pay.

There is little or no fun in loafing if you can't bother somebody who is busy.

Society Note— Mr. F.O. Bunkaby, of Argyll Court, left last evening by the west-bound for Banff, where he contemplates taking a bath.

LIES

Occasionally a man tells lies by keeping his mouth shut.

"They say" is the only excuse some people have for lying.

It's a waste of time telling a man he is a liar. If he is, he knows it.

Good liars are scarce but some liars are very skillful.

LIFE

Yes, to be sure, life may be a fleeting show, but it is the best show we have on earth.

All the world's a stage, and the majority of us sit in the gallery and throw things at the performers.

The science of living consists in not being a dead one.

Were it not for the things we are going to do, life would not be worth living.

The average man spends too much time making money and too little time enjoying it.

Life's sideshows cost us more than the real circus.

Make the best of your life. You will never get another chance to be happy.

Ever see the motto, "Live and Let Live," on the wall of a butcher shop?

As for the blind leading the blind, wouldn't it be hilarious to see those famous blinds, Blind Justice, Blind Cupid, and Blind Pig, trying to lead one another?

There are times when we should be thankful for what we fail to get.

The person who economizes his emotions, his money and his pleasures during his youth and middle age, gets about as much satisfaction out of life as a man who is dieting does out of his dinner.

Well, we have lived through the winter, those of us who have.

"*So you want to marry my daughter, eh?*" *said the experienced old gentleman.*

"*Yes sir.*"

"*Ever proposed before?*"

"*No sir.*"

"*Know much about women?*"

"*No sir.*"

"*Whew! Do you smoke?*"

"*No sir.*"

"*Drink much?*"

"*No sir.*"

"*Ever stayed out all night?*"

"*No sir.*"

"*Go away and learn something and come back in six months today.*"

LONELINESS

All the fun of staying out late at night is lost when there is nobody at home to make a fuss about it.

Gee! but this is an awful town,
*   Wherein to spend a Sunday;*
Nothing to do but mope and frown,
*   And live in hell till Monday!*

Nothing to drink and nothing to smoke,
*   Nowhere to go for amusement,*
Gee! but I wish I'd never woke,
*   To burden myself with such usement.*

Clear out, clear out, before it's too late,
*   You miserable, hardened old sinner,*
There's plenty more cities, at any rate,
*   Where they'll sell you a drink after dinner.*

Away to the land where they sell fat cigars,
*   And don't give a dam if it's Sunday,*

76

Away to the city with wide open bars,
Where they booze from Tuesday to Monday.

This is no place for a parson's son!
So, my friends, I leave you this ditty.
I'm going away to the Land of Fun,
To Hootch, the Blind Pig City.

LOVE

When a man is in love for the first time he thinks he invented it.

Some girls never find they have loved till after they are lost.

It is easier to love in spite of faults than because of virtues.

Say, here's a tip for you. Ink suitable for love letters and letters making dates is made of a solution of iodyde of starch. The writing fades away entirely in four weeks.

Every girl wants to marry rich. Girls don't believe in love as much as men suppose they do.

If we do not wrap up a little love with our Christmas gift what is the use?

It is a true saying that if you put two men in the same room, one with a toothache and the other in love, the man with the toothache will go to sleep first.

"I must fine you ten and costs," said the Magistrate, "for reckless driving."
"Listen, your honor!" pleaded the young motorist, "we were on our way to the parson to get married."
"Twenty-five dollars and costs. You're a darn sight more reckless than I thought you were."

The Father: "How is it sir, that I find you kissing my daughter? How is it, sir?"
The Nut: "Great, great!"

"Would you like me to come again on Monday night?" he
whispered lovingly to the dear creature on the front steps of
her ancestral home.

"Yes, do," she said shyly. *"I shall have nothing on that
night."*

MARRIAGE

"Marriage—ah—is a corporation of two persons with—ah
—power to increase its numbers—ah—so to speak."

Never judge a man by the opinion his wife has of him.

A married man imagines he is having a good time when
he does anything he knows his wife wouldn't approve of.

The only satisfaction some married women have is that
they are not old maids.

And the average married woman would doubtless spend
more money if her husband had any more to spend.

What has happened to the old-fashioned man who got on
his knees to propose?

A man wants a wife who can bake bread like her mother.
A woman wants a husband who can make dough like her
father.

The saddest and funniest thing on earth is to hear two
people promising at the altar with perfectly straight faces to
feel, think and believe for the rest of their lives exactly as
they do at that minute.

The only excuse some people have for marrying is that the
woman wants a home and the man wants a servant.

How it must jolt a man when he is polite to his wife in
public, to have her look as if she wasn't used to it.

Why is it that a big woman always takes a small man
seriously?

A woman's indifference has reached its limit if she no longer listens when her husband talks in his sleep.

Any girl can earn a good salary by marrying a poor man. True, she may not get it, but she'll earn it, all right.

When a woman can't think of anything else to say to her husband, she cautions him not to eat so much or smoke so much.

It doesn't take a girl's ideal long to develop into a commonplace and most diabolically dull husband.

Nothing else frightens a man so much as his wife's dead silence after he has failed to do the proper thing. It is like a stone wall with barbed wire on top. He can't get around it, nor see through it, or climb over it.

At this time of the year it is hard for a married man to understand why his wife should want to take ice and keep the furnace going at the same time.

Women sometimes feel unworthy of their husbands—in **books**.

A husband calls his wife "Birdie" because she is always associated in his mind with a bill.

When a man gets a letter from his wife during his absence from home, he simply reads the postscript and sends her a cheque.

Poor cookery may drive men to drink, but what drives 'em to poor cookery? We must get at the root of this matter.

Women are said never to be color blind, but then that were a small infliction compared to some other dismal defects. Just look at what some women marry!

After a man has been married three or four years the Romeo and Juliet balcony scene makes him weary.

Soon after marriage a girl's brain ceases to be a dream factory.

Married men always have more buttons off their clothes than bachelors.

Lot of wives don't know the value of money because they never see any.

The Stranger: "Are you quite sure that was a marriage license you gave me last month?"
The Official: "Of course! What's the matter?"
The Stranger: "I've lived a dog's life ever since."

Her hubby had been away from home for two or three months. The little wifey, shortly after his return, happened to be at an afternoon tea when the subject of conversation drifted on to pies—rhubarb pie, custard pie, blueberry pie, apple pie, peach pie and all sort of pie. As soon as she had a chance to get a word in edgeways, the little wifey broke in with:
"My husband is just crazy on pie. Do you know, when he got back home the other day, after being away for, oh, ever so long, the second thing he asked me for was a piece of apple pie."

Society Note— Skirts for the street should be as short as the police will allow. The shorter the better. Go to it. Don't mind us.

"I dreamt about you last night," said the husband in a surly voice.
"What did you dream?" asked his wife indifferently.
"I caught a man running away with you."
"And what did you say to him?"
"I asked him what he was running for."

MEEKNESS

Meanwhile, the meek are a long time inheriting the earth.

MEN

In this world of strife a man must be either an anvil or a hammer.

Two-thirds of all a man's troubles wear petticoats.

It's a fellow who wades in shallow water who stirs up most mud.

A man's true character crops out when he is dealing in triflles.

If you would make a tool of a man, select a dull one.

A boy is always a boy, but a man isn't always a man.

If men had to do the housework they would probably live in tents.

The average man is always paid average wages.

Our idea of a merciful man is one who puts a dog out of the room before starting the gramophone.

A married man can always afford anything he requires for his own use.

Why does a man invariably move the chair when he sits down?

If a man does not have the price of a meal about him he can always manage somehow to acquire a chew of tobacco.

Society Note— A charming souse was held last Sunday at the bungalow of Mr. James T. Runion, the well known leader of the bachelor set. The affair was quite informal.

MISFORTUNE

Misfortunes often put us wise to our own carelessness.

No man can appreciate the best of it until he has got the worst of it a few times. And don't we, the writer, know it!

If the wolf camps on your doormat, train him to chew up the bill collectors.

If a man is miserable it is usually because he thinks he is.

Most of life's shadows result from standing in our own light.

We know men who actually believe their troubles interest others.

Never kick a live wire when it is down.

When a man gets into trouble the majority of those who call to sympathize with him are only after particulars.

Men are like needles—when they are broke women have no use for them.

One of the worst stings of defeat is the sympathy that goes with it.

And most of our tragedies look comedies to our neighbors.

Nothing pleases some of us more than being able to convey bad news to others.

Learn to consume your own smoke. If you have hard luck or misfortunes, keep them to yourself.

Society Note— John Moran, of Sunnyside, who was killed last Wednesday by being run over by a Ford car was a good fellow and deserving of a more dignified death. There will be a sale of empty bottles at the Moran residence Saturday afternoon 2 o'clock, to defray the funeral expenses.

Society Note— Mr. John M. Alton, prominent business man of Calgary, was found dead in his cellar at his beautiful residence on Mount Royal last Tuesday. The spigot of 20-gallon keg of Old Glenlivet had been left open and the liquor had run all over the cellar floor. The many friends of the family feel deep sympathy for them in their terrible loss, which may be difficult to replace.

"*Who looks after you, my laddie?*"
"*Naebuddy.*"
"*Have you no father?*"
"*Father's deid.*"
"*And your mother?*"
"*No livin'.*"
"*No sister?*"
"*Naw.*"
"*Any brothers?*"
"*Ay, yin.*"
"*Well, can he not look after you! Where is he?*"
"*In Glesca College.*"
"*How long has he been there?*"
"*Three years.*"
"*Dear me, three years at the University, and can't help his little brother. What is he doing in the college?*"
"*Please, sir, he's in a bottle. He was born wi' twa heids.*"

MORALITY

The law should not impose standards of conduct that are not backed by public sentiment.

There is nothing better than a good woman and nothing worse than a bad one.

If only men could read women's thoughts they would take many more risks than they do.

Few of us are half so good, half so bad, half so poor, or half so rich as people imagine we are.

It's a bad thing to be a "good thing."

How a woman does enjoy doing for charity something that she thinks would be wicked to do for anything else.

Paying living wages to all women workers will not wipe out vice, but it will help.

Re the Carroll shooting case, in which Miss Lottie McCullough is charged with firing three bullets into Mr. Fred Carroll, it is expected that she will plead self-defense, on the ground that he shot one into her first.

Society Note— Another aldermanic candidate looms on the scene in the person of the Rev. W. Rufus, who is running on an uplift platform. Mr. Rufus is a trifle austere, inasmuch as he objects to drinking, smoking, dancing, theatres, card playing, horseracing and laughing. Otherwise he is all right. He is sure to be elected. Someone ought to teach Mr. Rufus how to shoot craps, to keep him from going crazy.

Smith had been out rooting at a baseball game and had shouted himself so hoarse that he could only talk in a faint whisper after the game. Desiring to tell his friend Jones all about the game, he called at Jones's house and Mrs. Jones came to the door.

"Is Jones in?" he whispered.

"No," whispered back Mrs. Jones. "Come in."

Society Note— Diamond Dolly has gone on a visit to the coast, leaving Miss Leta Long in full charge of her elegant dress-making parlors.

A man wished to introduce a friend to his wife at the seashore. When the pair got to the resort they found the wife in the surf. Entering the bathhouse the men donned their suits and went into the water. The husband introduced his friend.

A week later a friend observed the woman he had met in the water sitting opposite him in the street car. He bowed. She looked puzzled for a moment and then exclaimed:

"Oh, how do you do? I didn't know you with your clothes on."

They left the car at the next corner.

Miss Rosie Boote left on Tuesday's flier on a visit to friends in the East. We have not learned which of her young men is responsible for the trip, but he ought to be ashamed of himself.

"Don't you know," said the policeman to the servant, as she was dumping a pail of garbage in the open street, "that what you are doing is against the law?"

"Oh, don't talk to me about the law," replied the girl. "It's all I can do to keep the Ten Commandments!"

MOURNING

We always say that we don't want our friends to grieve after we are dead and gone—and they don't after the novelty wears off.

MUSIC

There is one redeeming feature about classical concerts. One never hears them whistled on the streets the next day.

When you hear a church choir singing: "There will be no more sorrow there," you conclude at once that either the aforementioned choir won't be there, or they won't be permitted to sing.

Society Note— Mrs. John Blogg, of Mount Royal, was hostess at a jolly tea last Wednesday. Mrs. B. presided at the table with her usual charming air of embonpoint and inebriety while old Blogg himself, who was far from sober, entertained the company with a few comic songs. Mrs. Blogg was assisted in pouring the tea by Miss Binkle, whose long experience in pouring beer stood her in good stead and made her task easy.

NEWSPAPERMEN

In trying to get up in the world, politicians use newspaper men as step ladders.

NEIGHBORS

As a matter of fact, your neighbors think just as disagreeable thoughts about you as you think about them.

When a woman plans to do anything out of the ordinary she always wonders what the neighbors will say.

A man is presumed to be guilty by his neighbors until he is proved innocent.

It doesn't cost half as much to live as it does to make a favorable impression on the neighbors.

"Yes," complained the pretty girl, who sat with her best fellow night after night on the porch, during the hot weather, "Mine is a hard lot. If I talk loud I annoy the neighbors and if I keep quiet it worries mother so."

For six years a bitter feud had existed between the Browns and the Robinsons, next door neighbors. The trouble had originated through the depredations of Brown's cat and had grown so fixed an affair that neither party ever dreamed of "making up." One day, however, Brown sent his servant with a peace-making note for Mr. Robinson, which read:

"Mr. Brown sends his compliments to Mr. Robinson, and begs to state that his old cat died this morning."

Robinson's reply was bitter:

"Mr. Robinson is sorry to hear of Mr. Brown's trouble, but he had not heard that Mrs. Brown was ill."

Society Note— A number of friends of Miss Annabel McSwattie, who is shortly to be married to Mr. J.B. Kipper, the well-known rancher of High River, gave her a delightful surprise party last Wednesday night. Judging from the complaints of neighbors, the function must have passed off very successfully. Miss McSwattie is one of our most popular debutantes and can carry an awful load without showing it, beyond an occasional yell or two. She is a star.

OPPORTUNITY

Opportunity does a great deal that ability gets the credit for.

It's an ill wind that doesn't blow things the lawyer's way.

OPTIMISM

An optimist says that good intentions are better than no pavements at all.

For that blue feeling try the sunny side of the street.

ORIGINALITY

Originality is merely a new way of expressing an old thought.

PATIENCE

Young man, never run after a streetcar, a woman or a real estate agent—there will be another along in a few minutes.

A beautiful answer was given by a little Scotch school girl. When her class was examined she was asked, "What is patience?"
Her reply was, "Wait a wee, and dinna weary."

PERFORMANCE

Saying of great men: "The bee that gets the honey doesn't loaf around the hive."

Quit making good resolutions and get down to business.

Society Note— William "Bill" McClusky, the eminent burnt cork comedian now playing the Pantages circuit, was the guest last Monday of the Pussyfoot Johnson Chapter of the Consecrated Bootleggers' Association. Mr. McClusky expressed the greatest admiration for Canada, but deplored the quality of the whiskey. This did not, however, deter Mr. McClusky from lapping up everything in sight. How he got through with his performance that night is a mystery to his many friends.

PERSUASION

You may succeed in convincing a man against his will but what's the use?

Society Note— Mr. J. Fuller Prunes, of Vancouver, is registered at the Palliser. He is trying to interest investors in Vancouver realty, but so far has only succeeded in arousing the interest of the house detective.

PESSIMISM

One confirmed pessimist rises to remark that the reason we mortals so distrust each other is that we are all so much alike.

Try a cool beer or long. Collins for your fit of pessimism. Why be poor when you can be rich for half a dollar?

PLAY

Play is merely work that you don't have to do.

POLITICS

Politics is the greatest riddle of all.

One is forced to the conclusion that there is too much politics in politics.

It is the terrible man that has nothing and wants nothing that is most feared in politics.

Politics, you will observe, is the science of guessing right.

Politics is a good game, but a mighty poor business.

What a politician says is one thing and what he does is another.

Political success is like a flea—now you see it, now you don't.

Politicians these days are being divided into two classes—appointed and disappointed.

Some day there will be an investigation of the high cost of investigations.

It is a mighty poor politician who cannot promise his friends and supporters anything they want.

Why is it that all the rogues manage to get into the other political party?

Some fellow made the remark the other day that there was small difference between the Liberal and the Conservative parties. There is all the difference in the world. One is in and the other is out.

One of the consoling things about public life is that no matter what kind of a spectacular ass a man may make of himself in public matters, he will always receive a stack of letters commending his course.

A propos Liberal and Conservative parties: of two evils it is best to choose neither.

Most of any government's troubles come from trying to uphold the blunders it makes.

Society Note— Premier Meighen has decided not to extend his western tour beyond Moose Jaw. The expense of the dining car on this tour has drained the Liberal Conservative exchequer and his party are now living on crackers and cheese. This is a bum diet to speak on. Up to Tuesday it had been thought that they might have crackered and cheesed it as far as Medicine Hat, but God willed otherwise.

Society Note— Hon. Crothers, Minister of Labor, has accepted an alluring offer to go into vaudeville, and will appear at Pantages very shortly in monologue. His contract calls for a 15-minute humorous talk on his administration of the Labor department. It should elicit considerable laughter.

Popular opinion is the most fickle thing on earth.

POPULARITY

If you would be popular you must be a good forgetter.

It may be what people don't know about a popular man that makes him popular.

Speaking of popularity, there is also the damfool with a pretty sister.

Society Note— Miss Tessie Blink, the talented daughter of old man Blink, leaves next week for her father's farm near Okotoks, where she will take up the study of milking cows and doing chores. Miss Blink's many friends will regret her departure. Mrs. Toodleums poured the tea, assisted by Miss Grundlewhackster.

A well-known and popular young doctor was at a dinner party recently and the conversation veered around to the rapid growth of the city.

"Yes," said the doctor, "since I've been here there have been no less than six hundred births."

"Don't you think," observed a guest quietly from across the table, "that it's about time you were taking a rest?"

POVERTY

A poor man is one who gets his money by earning it.

The most miserable chap in the world is the poor man with a rich man's vices.

In this land of plenty they are plenty of people who haven't.

The man who is too poor to lend money to his friends will never have many enemies.

Governments of the world are learning among other things that the people want to eat with considerable regularity.

It is hard for a man to support sealskin on a muskrat salary.

A poor man is always saying he would like to be rich, because of the great amount of good he could do with the money. Awful bunk, eh?

Someone said that wealth does not beget contentment. We are quite positive that poverty doesn't. And there you are.

"Well, my little man," said the kindly old lady to a very lonesome looking kid, *"and who is your father?"*
"Ain't got none."
"Poor boy. And who is your mother?"
"Never had any."
"Bless my soul, who are you anyway?"
"I'm a mean trick that was played on auntie."

Society Note— The rumor that Peter McGiggle, the well-known pin pool expert and society leader, had been given up by his doctors is only partly true. They had only given him up as a hopeless bankrupt and therefore did not operate. Mr. McGiggle's many friends will be delighted to learn that he is now quite well.

PRIDE

Few men are able to appreciate getting the short end of a joke.

When a man is ill he seldom has a night shirt pretty enough to receive callers in.

After a girl gets to be so old, she makes a bonfire of the baby picture of herself taken in a wash bowl.

PROHIBITION

One advantage of prohibition is that you no longer hear the pet grievance which men unload on you after the third drink.

Society Note— Rev. Captain Bob Pearson returned to Calgary from France this week and expressed himself as delighted over the rigorous enforcement of the liquor laws. He should be taken around to The Bear's Den on Sixth Avenue East, behind the church.

"If any man here," shouted the temperance orator, "Can name an honest business that has been helped by the bar I will spend the rest of my life working for the liquor people."

A man in the audience arose.

"I consider my business an honest one," he said, "and it has been helped by the bar."

"What is your business?" yelled the orator.

"I, sir," responded the man, "am an undertaker."

PRUDES

Prudes are women who are always looking for temptations to resist.

A prude is a girl who always knows a lot of things she shouldn't know.

RELIGION

The Salvation Army is religion with its coat off.

The man who uses religion as a cloak in this world may have more use for a smoking jacket in the next.

How many men do you know who let their religion interfere with their business?

When a man mixes religion with politics the religion is apt to lose its identity.

How many clergymen believe all they preach?

The minister hurried down the aisle and grasped the stranger's hand.

"I'm glad to see you with us to-night," he said. "I can see by the expression of your face that you are laboring under some deep sorrow, some great disappointment."

"You're right; I came in here thinking it was a movie and having got in, I didn't have the nerve to get up and walk out."

Society Note— John P. Quigley, the local evangelist, who fell into an open sewer and broke his flask, has fully recovered and is now able to be about.

REMORSE

Remorse is memory that has begun to ferment.

REPUTATION

Character is what you are. Reputation is what you try to make people think you are.

Some men spend half their lives in making a reputation and the other half in trying to live it down. Vide ourself.

SADNESS

Gladness is appreciated only by those who know what sadness is.

In order to enjoy life a man must be a little miserable occasionally.

SARCASM

How much does it cost you each year to be sarcastic?

Sneers are the weapons of helpless fools.

A certain Baron, who was a bit of a snob, was addressing his constituents at a meeting which, as usual, had an Irishman "in its midst."

"My friends," exclaimed the Baron, "my title is of no mushroom growth. My grandfather was a Baron, my father was a Baron ...."

"It's a great pity yer mother wasn't Baron too!" shouted the Irishman.

SAVINGS

Money that a man has saved represents the good times he didn't have.

SIN

Many a good man who condemns a sinner secretly envies him.

A man who looks like a sinner to other men may look like a saint to some woman.

To do right is easy when sin ceases to be a pleasure.

It is the things we shouldn't do that seem to make life worth living.

The young lad came home to dinner and in the course of conversation his father discovered that he was $5 shy in some collections he had been making.

"What did you do with the money?" asked the stern parent.

"Well, to tell the truth, I was walking along the street and a girl called me into the house."

"A girl? What girl?"

"Oh, she had blonde hair. That's all I know about her."

"Oh, ho!" said the stern parent with a faint grin. "And how did you make out?"

"Say, dad," said the youngster, reaching for the mustard, "if I was Andrew Carnegie I'd make a hobby of that."

Miss Maggie McCheese, who wrote to us from an address in East Calgary, complaining about a certain young man who tried to kiss her, may be consoled to learn that the fellow says he would not have attempted such a thing had he been sober. He further offers the opinion that Maggie's mouth is merely a hole in her face for pie. We hope that Miss McCheese will accept this explanation and let the matter drop.

SPECULATION

All the speculation in the world never raised a bushel of wheat.

SPEECH

Never use the expression, "It makes me sick." It doesn't sound well.

SPINSTERS

The difference between a bachelor girl and an old maid is that a bachelor girl has never been married, and an old maid has never been married, or anything.

Two dear old ladies were discussing husbands.

Said the first, "I have been married three times. Each of my husbands are dead, though. They were all cremated."

Her friend was a dear old maiden lady.

She listened attentively to her friend, and when she had concluded the sad story of her life, she said:

"How wonderful are the ways of providence. Here I've lived all these years and have never been able to get one husband and you've had husbands to burn."

Every man realizes that he used to be a chump. (Faint applause.)

Some men and women are like silver plated knives. They look bright, but they are usually dull.

It's difficult to convince a man that he's a chump—and if you do, what's the use?

If many people were to think before they speak they would forget what they were going to say.

Many a fellow has more money than brains, who isn't rich, either.

If some men (and women) were to refrain from telling what they don't know it would be a great surprise to their acquaintances.

"What is this man charged with?"
"Bigotry, your honor. He's got three wives."

SUCCESS

The proof of success is the ability to deliver the goods.

Every successful man knows more about his own business than he does about other men's.

Too many salt away money in the brine of other people's tears.

It always makes a man peevish when people compliment him on his success and then add that they can't understand it.

Blessed be the oil! Calgary has now become famous for something besides being the place where Calgary beer comes from.

The most successful farmers seem to be editors of agricultural papers.

102

A successful man is one whom everybody claims to have known when he didn't have a pot to—er—gimme a match—cook beans in.

The less a man knows the more suspicious he is.

A woman is always suspicious of another woman who dresses better than herself.

A woman is more influenced by what she suspects than by what she is told.

If wives don't want to catch their husbands in mischief they shouldn't watch them.

Society Note— A bouncing ten-pound boy arrived at the home of Mr. and Mrs. P.T. Gilpin, of Fifteenth Avenue West, last Tuesday. Mr. Gilpin has fired the hired man and engaged a more aged servitor.

Why does the Calgary Herald *insert ads like this in its columns?*
"Gentleman, slightly affected with sciatica, wishes the services of a young or middle-aged woman for massage purposes. Must give treatment at her own apartment or home."

The late Judge Travis was a wealthy man but dreadfully close in money matters and very, very suspicious. During one of the land booms a couple of local real estate agents called on him to try and interest him in a certain scheme of theirs. They talked to him for about an hour. Then they took their leave.

"I believe we've got him," said the first real estate man, hopefully.
"I don't know," said the other. "He seems very suspicious."
"Suspicious? What makes you think that?"
"Didn't you notice how he counted his fingers after I had shaken hands with him?"

TEARS

One of the things it is impossible for a man to understand is why a woman cries when there is no reason for it and doesn't cry when there is.

If a woman cries after quarreling with her husband, it's because she thought of something mean she might have said but didn't think of it in time.

One of the mysteries that man has so far failed to solve is the reason why a woman cries when she is glad.

TELEPHONE

Trying to guess who it is when the telephone rings provides the average woman with lots of excitement.

You can't judge a woman by her telephone voice.

TEMPTATION

A man seldom attempts to escape any temptation that looks good to him.

Good men, like good women, never see temptation when they meet it.

Fresh light on the Eden story. Eve was so easily tempted because she wanted to get some clothes.

Oh well, speaking of certain cabarets, it's hard for most of us to be good when we have a chance not to be.

"Why don't you do as you did when you came home last night, John?"
"How was that?"
"Why, when I met you in the dark hallway you caught me in your arms and kissed me."
"Gee, was that you?"

Society Note— George B. McCoole, who has been running around with a bottle soliciting votes for his aldermanic campaign, called at this office and wanted his picture in the paper. If McCoole will bring up another bottle and not take it away as he did the other one, we will give the matter our prayerful consideration.

THRIFT

Thrift is what a man has to practice so that his wife may be extravagant. (Loud cheers and voice—"Thazzo, thazzo!")

TIME

Time is said to magnify our good deeds and diminsh our naughty ones. (Important, if true.—Ed.)

TROUBLE

Have you ever noticed how much larger your troubles appear at night than during the day?

The shadow of trouble is usually blacker than the trouble itself.

TRUTH

Truth is mighty—mighty scarce.

You are what you are only when no one is looking.

There is nothing hypocritical about the wagging of a dog's tail.

To transform friends into enemies simply tell the whole truth about them.

Is not this the truth? Few people to whom you are introduced really care to know you.

Some men spoil a good story by sticking to the facts.

A woman is never too good to be true. (Loud and prolonged cheers.)

The individual who tells the truth with deliberate carefulness isn't believed half so often as a fellow who can lie gracefully.

VANITY

Vanity isn't on the official list of virtues, yet unless a man has a good opinion of himself he will never amount to much.

What a slovenly old world this would be if all the vanity were eliminated.

VICE

The way of the transgressor is very popular.

Tobacco is next on the programme of the society for the suppression of vice in others.

When a man is smoking it adds to his enjoyment if his wife worries for fear he will drop ashes on the carpet.

Society Note — Peter McSorley has returned to the city after a prolonged visit to the Edmonton penitentiary.

"These photographs you made of myself and husband are not at all satisfactory and I refuse to accept them. Why, my husband looks like an ape!"

"Well, madam, that's no fault of mine. You should have thought of that before you had him taken."

VINDICTIVENESS

Women have a clever way of saying mean things that men can never hope to equal.

The man who harbors a grudge and forgets favors is the most undesirable of all citizens.

How one woman must hate another when she speaks of her as "that thing."

A woman has as many ways of making a man feel cheap as she has of using up stale bread.

VOLUBILITY

It is unwise to measure a man's intellect by the volubility of speech.

It is as easy to talk as it is difficult to say something.

You can't judge a man's brain power by his tongue power.

The man who can talk without saying anything is the one who shines in society. Two jumps, please.

A woman always has the last word—and, incidently, about ninety percent of the preceding conversation.

Ever notice how little attention is paid to people who talk too much?

When most people talk they waste a lot of valuable time in giving unnecessary details.

We admire a good talker who knows when to shut up.

The tongue, like a race horse, generally runs faster the less weight it carries.

Many a woman's idea of a bore is a man who talks as if he had good sense.

Some men never weary of talking about the things they used to do.

While the world is studying control of the air, someone should arrange for control of hot air.

When a woman says, "There's no use talking," she means that you might as well shut up and give her a chance.

Some men are pleasant enough to talk to, but rather disagreeable to listen to.

The louder a man talks the easier it is to discredit anything he says.

Society Note— Organizer McSwattie, of Minneapolis, arrived last night to try and settle the dispute between the Golf Caddies' Union (Calgary branch) and the municipal golf course authorities. He will meet the Commissioners this afternoon. A strike is imminent. Mr. ScSwattie is accompanied by a blind secretary, who was talked into loss of his eyesight by his loquacious boss.

WEALTH

Wealth is not his who gets it, but his who enjoys it.

Grey matter is all right in its place—and so is the long green.

How many make a million?
Not many.

The world doesn't care if a man is short of brains provided he is long on money.

That man has "arrived" financially who has reached the stage where he puts on a clean collar without looking to see whether the old one is dirty.

Passing thought on Labor day:
Labor is the foundation of many a fortune—but not necessarily of the laborers.

Cheer up! It cannot last forever. Money will reappear as suddenly and mysteriously as it disappeared. Don't get alarmed. Be calm. Keep cool. Tell the man in the white jacket to mix you a Scotch highball and look pleasant.

Someone sends us the query, "when is a man rich?"

It is hard to say. Perhaps we might hazard the guess that it is when he has about fifteen drinks under his belt and 75 cents left.

WEATHER

One would not object to Alberta's climate changing, if it didn't change oftener than twice a day.

WHISKEY

Time was when some whiskey was better than other whiskey. Now some whiskey is worse than other whiskey.

Society Note— Peter O'Snuffigan, of Crossfield, who got lost on the prairie during last week's snowstorm while out campaigning for Candidate Moore, has contracted a terrible cold. He says it serves him right.

The evangelist stopped and gravely inquired of the passer-by if he were ready to die. The latter replied that he had not thought much about it.

"But every time I breathe, a man dies," solemnly remarked the evangelist in tones of terrible warning.

"Then why don't you chew a few cloves!"

She said to the young man: "I wouldn't want to marry a man who smoked or drank, or played cards, or belonged to clubs, or stayed out at night. Of course I would want him to have a good time."

"Where?" asked the young man.

WISDOM

The world may be growing wiser, but we still have a lot to learn.

Solomon had a world-wide reputation for wisdom, but then the old gentleman had never served on a city council.

A man has reached the age of discretion when he is willing to admit that other men may have opinions different from his without being fools.

One trouble with most of our brilliant thoughts is that they were original with the ancient thinkers.

Instead of doing things today, the wise man did them yesterday.

Don't tell all you know; keep a little for seed.

It sometimes happens that a boy learns some very good habits by not following in the footsteps of his father.

A man's head is like his pocketbook. It's not the outside appearance, but what it contains that counts.

Wise is the man who is never as funny as he can be.

Training will do much for a man, but it will not teach him to look for the towel before filling his eyes with soap.

Wisdom is the art of being out when people call to make a touch.

A man who acknowledges that he is a chump has begun to acquire wisdom.

Society Note— Miss Pearl Raymore left for Macleod by Tuesday's southbound. A general hope is expressed in police circles that she will stay there.

A young man, an only son, married against his parents' wishes. Afterward, in telling a friend how to break the news to them, he said:
"Start off by telling them that I am dead, and then gently work up to the climax."

A rich man, lying on his death bed, called his chauffeur who had been in his service for years, and said:
"Ar, Sykes. I am going on a long and rugged journey, worse than you ever drove me."

"Well, sir," consoled the chauffeur, "there's one comfort. It's all down-hill."

WOMEN

And there are also a few women who don't understand men.

If her heart is in the right place it matters not whether a woman is younger or older than she looks.

She is a wise woman who is known by the company she declines to keep.

The most extraordinary peculiarity about women is that the more a man knows about them the more he has to learn.

A girl of sixteen pretends to know a lot more than a woman of thirty will admit she knows.

Girls with the most cheek do the least blushing.

If a man understands one woman he should let it go at that.

Women remind us of angels because they are always flying around.

No doubt about it at all. Eve was the real inventor of the loose leaf system.

A woman never feels dressed up unless she feels uncomfortable.

Why does a woman always turn her back on her companion when she opens her purse?

Few women are deep thinkers—but they are all clothes observers. (Help! Help!)

Never judge a woman by the company she is compelled to entertain.

Society Note— Mrs. J. B. Clinktwister, 2896 Twenty-eighth Ave. East, will receive the first Thursday of every month, the second Tuesday of every week, the fourth Friday before the last Saturday, and the second last Wednesday before each Monday.

> *Oh, woman of the shifting shape,*
> *Victim of ill-jest and jape,*
> *When there's no target for our wit*
> *Then, beautiful angel, you are "it."*

Women apparently can stand the cold much better than men. During the recent cold snap we overheard one lady say to another that she would be over that evening if she had nothing on.

Society Note— Mrs. J.P. Scufflesnorter gave one of her charming Fine Old Scotch socials at Tripe Court last Tuesday afternoon. Mr. John Irvine, candidate for West Calgary, was present and gave the ladies a song and dance. The gathering broke up in a row.

WOMEN'S SUFFRAGE

Events in the legislature suggest the well-known toast, "Here is to woman, once our superior, now our equal."

This suffragatte nonsense makes us very tired. There is only one way to head it off. Make the legal age for voting thirty-five instead of twenty-one.

Apropos of the proposed women's suffrage in Alberta, we must fain admit that the women will (in all probability) not be more careless in electing the wrong candidates than the men have been at various times.

The Liberals are kicking because every woman in Canada is not being enfranchised. We never took overmuch stock in giving women the franchise out and out, because women will always vote just as their male relatives or friends want them to. All they really want with the vote is to trade it for masculine approval. (We will now proceed to bend our head to the storm. Go easy!)

It appears that women are eligible to sit on our city council. It also appears that they don't want to, particularly. You see, it's this way—the word "alderman" is merely a corruption of "older man" and it would be too much to expect the office to become popular with alderwomen.

WORK

It is a pity that man who invented work never finished it.

WORRY

Whatever else you do with a worry, don't pass it on.

Yesterday's neglect causes two-thirds of today's worries.

Sources

INTRODUCTION— 1. Eye Opener, June 15, 1907; 2. EO, June 29, 1906; 3. EO, Sept. 16, 1911; 4. Reprinted in Calgary *Herald,* April 4, 1898; 5. EO, March 4, 1905; 6. EO, Feb. 25, 1905; 7. For a biography of Edwards see *The Best of Bob Edwards,* edited by Hugh A. Dempsey (Hurtig Publishers, 1975); 8. EO, March 5, 1910; 9. EO, June 18, 1910; 10. EO, Jan. 1, 1910; 11. Summer Annual, 1924, 33; 12. EO, Jan. 25, 1919; 13. Summer Annual, 1924, 52; 14. EO, Nov. 20, 1915; 15. *Familiar Quotations,* by John Bartlett (Little, Brown & Co., Boston, 1937), 962; 16. EO, Dec. 21, 1912; 17. *Familiar Quotations,* 994; 18. EO, May 17, 1913; 19. *Familiar Quotations,* 1044; 20. EO, Feb. 10, 1912; 21. EO, Dec. 21, 1912; 22. EO, May, 4, 1912; 23, Summer Annual, 1922, 39; 24. EO, Aug. 20, 1921; 25. EO, Feb. 5,1921; 26. EO, Oct. 19, 1918; 27. EO, June 25, 1921; 28. Summer Annual, 1922, 29.

ACCURACY— EO, Jan. 6, 1917. ADVERSITY— EO, June 28, 1919; EO, Nov. 24, 1917. ADVICE— EO, Dec. 11, 1920. AGE— EO, Feb. 17, 1917; Summer Annual, 1920, 80; Summer Annual, 1922, 63; EO, Oct. 23, 1911; EO, Nov. 19, 1921; EO, Nov. 24, 1917; EO, May 15, 1920; EO, Oct. 2, 1920; EO, July 1, 1922. AMBITION— EO, July 3, 1915; EO, March 15, 1919; EO, July 26, 1919; EO, May 22, 1915; EO, March 9, 1912; EO, Nov. 20, 1915; EO, April 3, 1915; EO, March 23, 1912. AMERICANS— EO, Sept. 16, 1911; EO, June 5, 1920; EO, Feb. 19, 1921. ANGER— EO, Feb. 2, 1918; EO, Aug. 28, 1920; EO, March 20, 1915; EO, Nov. 19, 1921. APPLAUSE— EO, Aug. 14, 1920. APPRECIATION— EO, May 28, 1921; EO, June 27, 1914. ARGUMENT— EO, Feb. 19, 1921; EO, April 5, 1919; EO, July 17, 1920; EO, Dec. 11, 1920; EO, April 10, 1920; Summer Annual, 1922, 39; EO, Nov. 1, 1919. AUTOMOBILES— EO, July 1, 1922; EO, June 6, 1914; EO, July 17, 1920.

BACHELORS— EO, Dec. 11, 1920; EO, Nov. 24, 1917; EO, Sept. 27, 1913; EO, Sept. 1, 1917; EO, March 24, 1913. BANKRUPTCY— EO, Nov. 8, 1913. BAR-ROOM— EO, June 12, 1915. BEAUTY— Summer Annual, 1923, 37; EO, Feb. 26, 1916; EO, Oct. 5, 1918; EO, Nov. 18, 1911; Summer Annual, 1923, 18. BLUFF— EO, March 31, 1911; Summer Annual, 1923, 86; EO, Aug. 6, 1910. BOASTFULNESS— Summer Annual, 1921, 35; EO, Feb. 22, 1919; EO, Dec. 12, 1914. BOOZE— EO, Feb. 19, 1910; EO, Dec. 6, 1919; EO, Aug. 23, 1919; EO, April 20, 1912; EO, May 22, 1915; EO, May 11, 1918; EO, March 9, 1918; EO, Jan. 22, 1921; EO, June 5, 1920; EO, March 20, 1915; Summer Annual, 1923, 84; Summer Annual, 1923, 53; EO, July 17, 1920; EO, June 17, 1916; Summer Annual, 1921, 15; EO, Dec. 11, 1920; EO, May 15, 1920; EO, Aug. 23, 1919.

CEREMONY— Summer Annual, 1923, 8. CHILDREN— EO, May 28, 1921; EO, Dec. 3, 1921; EO, Nov. 18, 1911. CIVILIZATION— EO, July 15, 1911; EO, Oct. 13, 1917; EO, Feb. 8, 1919; EO, Feb. 2, 1918; EO, Nov. 16, 1912; EO, Oct. 23, 1915; EO, Aug. 9, 1919; EO, Sept. 16, 1911. CLEVERNESS— EO, April 20, 1918; EO, Aug. 28, 1915. CONCEIT— EO, Aug. 2, 1913; EO, Feb. 19, 1921; EO, Sept. 1, 1920; EO, May 22, 1915; EO, July 20, 1918; EO, Feb. 26, 1916; EO, Aug. 3, 1912; EO, April 8, 1916; Summer Annual, 1921, 81; EO, Feb. 5, 1921; EO, Aug. 28, 1915; EO, May 6, 1916; Summer Annual, 1923, 56; EO, Oct. 2, 1920; EO, April 12, 1913. CONSCIENCE— Summer Annual, 1924, 33; EO, Aug. 26, 1915; Summer Annual, 1923, 85; EO, April 6, 1912; EO, Jan. 22, 1921; EO, Nov. 18, 1911. CONTENTMENT— EO, Feb. 11, 1911; EO, Feb. 19, 1921; EO, March 9, 1918; EO, June 3, 1911; EO, April 3, 1915. CONTRARY-MINDEDNESS— EO, June 12, 1915; Summer Annual, 1923, 66; EO, Aug. 23, 1919. COURAGE— EO, Dec. 3, 1921; EO, Jan. 13, 1912; EO, Aug. 14, 1920. CREDIT— EO, March 14, 1914; EO, Dec. 6, 1919; EO, Oct. 23, 1915; EO, Oct. 11, 1919; EO, Aug. 23, 1919; EO, June 27, 1914; EO, June 29, 1918. CRITICISM— EO, Sept. 1, 1917; EO, April 20, 1918; EO, Nov. 3, 1917; EO, April 8, 1916. CRITICS— Summer Annual, 1923, 56; EO, March 30, 1917. CURIOSITY— EO, May 11, 1918; EO, June 25, 1921; EO, May 8, 1915; EO, Sept. 22, 1917; EO, Aug. 2, 1913; EO, March 20, 1915. CYNICISM— EO, March 14, 1914; EO, Jan. 25, 1919; EO, Nov. 22, 1919; Summer Annual, 1923, 66.

DEATH— EO, March 14, 1914; EO, April 30, 1921; EO, March 15, 1919; EO, July 29, 1911; EO, Nov. 21, 1914; EO, Feb. 19, 1921; EO, Oct. 14, 1916; EO, March 6, 1920; EO, Sept. 1, 1917. DIGNITY— EO, May 6, 1916. DILLUSION— EO, Dec. 11, 1920. DIPLOMACY— EO, Aug. 23, 1919; EO, June 29, 1918; EO, Nov. 22, 1919; EO, Sept. 1, 1920; Summer Annual, 1923, 64; EO, Sept. 13, 1919; EO, March 20, 1920; EO, March 30, 1918. DISCOURAGEMENT— EO, Aug. 20, 1921; Summer Annual, 1923, 78; Summer Annual, 1921, 15. DISHONESTY— EO, March 20, 1915; EO, Sept. 22, 1917; EO, Feb. 8, 1919; EO, Oct. 23, 1915; EO, April 8, 1916; EO, Oct. 23, 1920; EO, May 8, 1915; EO, Dec. 25, 1920; Summer Annual, 1924, 1; EO, Oct. 23, 1920; EO, June 5, 1920. DISSATISFACTION— EO, Feb. 19, 1921; EO, Feb. 26, 1916; EO, June 5, 1920; EO, April 20, 1912. DOCTORS— EO, May 8, 1915; EO, May 6, 1916; EO, Nov. 16, 1912. DOUBTS— Summer Annual, 1921, 77; EO, Dec. 20, 1913; EO, Feb. 5, 1921. DRUGS— EO, May 31, 1919. DRUNKENNESS— EO, May 22, 1915; EO, June 12, 1915; EO, March 31, 1911; EO, Sept. 7, 1912; EO, May 17, 1913; EO, Oct. 11, 1919; EO, Sept. 16, 1911; Summer Annual, 1922, 91; EO, Aug. 2, 1913; EO, June 28, 1919; EO, Feb. 26, 1916; EO, Aug. 28, 1915; Summer Annual, 1923, 55; EO, March 20, 1915. DUPLICITY— EO, Aug. 30, 1913; EO, June 25, 1921; EO, May 6, 1916; EO, Dec. 11, 1915; EO, Aug. 23, 1919; EO, Sept. 1, 1917; EO, May 12, 1919; Summer Annual, 1923, 78; EO, March 20, 1915; EO, March 20, 1920; EO, June 29, 1918.

ECONOMY— EO, May 13, 1922. EFFICIENCY— EO, June 12, 1915; EO, June 8, 1912. ELOQUENCE— EO, March 14, 1914. ENEMIES— EO, Oct. 2, 1920; EO, Oct. 23, 1915; EO, Dec. 8, 1917; EO, May 15, 1920; EO, May 22, 1915; EO, May 27, 1916; EO, July 1, 1922. ENVY— EO, April 20, 1918. EVIL— EO, Dec. 17, 1921. EXPECTATIONS— EO, Oct. 23, 1920; Summer Annual, 1921, 86.

FAILURE— EO, March 29, 1913; EO, Aug. 28, 1915; EO, Jan. 25, 1919. FAITH— EO, June 29, 1918; Summer Annual, 1923, 53; EO, May 28, 1921. FAME— EO, May 6, 1911; EO, March 14, 1914; EO, June 5, 1920; EO, Feb. 26, 1916; EO, May 22, 1915; EO, July 29, 1922. FASHION— EO, March 31, 1911; EO, Nov. 21, 1914; EO, Feb. 22, 1919; EO, March 30, 1917; EO, July 17, 1920; EO, June 17, 1916; EO, Feb. 17, 1917; EO, June 12, 1915; EO, Dec. 2, 1916; Summer Annual, 1923, 65; EO, May 6, 1916; EO,

Oct. 23, 1920. FLATTERY— EO, Feb. 7, 1919; EO, Oct. 23, 1915; EO, Nov. 16, 1912; EO, Sept. 27, 1913; Summer Annual, 1923, 62. FOOLISHNESS— EO, April 3, 1915; EO, Nov. 21, 1914; EO, April 25, 1914; Summer Annual, 1923, 83; Summer Annual, 1923, 73; EO, Oct. 11, 1919; EO, Jan. 22, 1921; EO, Oct. 5, 1912; EO, Jan. 1, 1910; EO, Nov. 3, 1917; EO, Oct. 2, 1920. FRIENDSHIP— EO, March 6, 1920; EO, July 3, 1915; EO, Aug. 14, 1920; EO, May 15, 1920; EO, Jan. 13, 1912; EO, Aug. 20, 1921; EO, Nov. 1, 1919; EO, Oct. 23, 1915; EO, April 20, 1912; EO, Sept. 22, 1917; EO, Sept. 7, 1912; Summer Annual, 1923, 55; EO, Nov. 19, 1921; EO, Dec. 20, 1913; EO, Aug. 28, 1915; EO, May 12, 1919; EO, May 11, 1918; EO, March 20, 1915; EO, Nov. 2, 1912; Summer Annual, 1923, 24. FRUSTRATION— EO, Dec. 3, 1921; EO, June 11, 1921; EO, March 20, 1920. FUSSINESS— EO, Aug. 28, 1920; EO, Oct. 11, 1919; EO, Aug. 3, 1912.

GAMBLING— EO, Dec. 11, 1915; EO, May 12, 1919; Summer Annual, 1921, 67; EO, May 12, 1919. GENEROSITY— EO, Feb. 26, 1916. GLUTTONY— EO, March 14, 1914; EO, March 20, 1915; EO, May 22, 1915; Summer Annual, 1923, 37. GOLF— Summer Annual, 1920, 60; Summer Annual, 1921, 29; EO, May 12, 1919; EO, Dec. 6, 1919. GOODNESS— EO, Feb. 22, 1919; EO, Aug. 28, 1920; EO, Nov. 22, 1919; EO, Jan. 6, 1917; EO, June 12, 1915; EO, Nov. 21, 1914; EO, Nov. 8, 1913; EO, March 30, 1918; EO, Dec. 11, 1915; EO, Feb. 25, 1905. GOOD DEEDS— EO, Nov. 20, 1915. GOSSIP— EO, Nov. 22, 1919; EO, April 30, 1921; EO, April 30, 1921; April 30, 1921; EO, March 9, 1918; EO, Dec. 30, 1911; EO, Aug. 14, 1920; EO, Nov. 22, 1919; EO, May 27, 1916; EO, June 11, 1921; EO, May 31, 1919; EO, May 31, 1919; EO, Aug. 28, 1915; EO, Dec. 30, 1913; EO, Dec. 21, 1912; EO, June 6, 1914; EO, Feb. 19, 1921; EO, June 28, 1919; EO, Sept. 1, 1917. GRAFT— Summer Annual, 1923, 10; EO, May 6, 1916. GREED— EO, June 5, 1920. GUILE— EO, July 17, 1920; EO, Dec. 11, 1915; Summer Annual, 1923, 18; EO, Aug. 2, 1913. GULLIBILITY— EO, Jan. 27, 1917; EO, March 9, 1912; EO, May 31, 1919; EO, Nov. 22, 1919; EO, Nov. 18, 1911.

HAPPINESS— EO, Aug. 23, 1919; Summer Annual, 1924, 11; Summer Annual, 1923, 62; EO, March 20, 1915; EO, Sept. 21, 1918; EO, Nov. 19, 1921; EO, Oct. 2, 1920; Summer Annual, 1922, 84; EO, March 20, 1920; EO, Jan. 25, 1919; EO, Sept. 16,

1911; EO, Jan. 22, 1921; EO, Dec. 20, 1919; Summer Annual, 1923, 31. HIGHBROW— EO, April 8, 1916. HISTORY— EO, May 31, 1919; EO, May 27, 1916. HOMES— EO, May 4, 1912; EO, March 20, 1915; EO, April 12, 1913. HONESTY— EO, Oct. 23, 1920; EO, Oct. 19, 1912; EO, April 8, 1916; Summer Annual, 1921, 53; EO, March 14, 1914; EO, Feb. 26, 1916; Summer Annual, 1921, 14; Summer Annual, 1922, 63; EO, April 12, 1913; EO, Sept. 1, 1917; EO, May 11, 1918. HUMOR— EO, Nov. 1, 1919; EO, May 22, 1915; EO, Sept. 24, 1921; EO, Sept. 7, 1912; EO, Dec. 12, 1914; EO, Sept. 22, 1917; EO, Oct. 23, 1911.

IGNORANCE— EO, Nov. 3, 1917; EO, Dec. 25, 1920; EO, Feb. 5, 1921; EO, Oct. 23, 1920; EO, Oct. 2, 1920; EO, May 11, 1918; EO, Dec. 6, 1919; EO, Sept. 22, 1917; EO, Sept. 7, 1912; EO, Oct. 14, 1916; EO, Nov. 1, 1919. ILLUSIONS— EO, June 17, 1916; Summer Annual, 1923, 191. INDEPENDENCE— Summer Annual, 1921, 16. INFLATION— EO, Dec. 6, 1919; EO, Dec. 11, 1920; EO, Feb. 17, 1917; EO, Oct. 11, 1919; EO, April 10, 1920. INGENUITY— EO, Dec. 1, 1915. INSPIRATION— Summer Annual, 1922, 32. INTELLI-GENCE— EO, May 22, 1915; EO, Feb. 11, 1911; EO, June 5, 1920.

KISSES— EO, Nov. 2, 1912. KNOWLEDGE— EO, Nov. 18, 1911; EO, Feb. 2, 1918; EO, May 8, 1915; EO, Aug. 2, 1913; EO, Sept. 22, 1917.

LAUGHTER— EO, Feb. 10, 1912; EO, April 25, 1914; EO, Dec. 11, 1920; EO, May 11, 1918; EO, March 30, 1917; EO, Feb. 26, 1916; EO, Aug. 28, 1920; EO, May 11, 1918; EO, Dec. 21, 1912. LAZINESS— Summer Annual, 1923, 35; EO, May 15, 1920; EO, Jan. 22, 1921; EO, Oct. 5, 1912. LEAP YEAR— EO, April 8, 1916; Summer Annual, 1923, 56. LEISURE— EO, Sept. 1, 1920; EO, June 29, 1918; EO, Oct. 2, 1920; EO, Nov. 3, 1917; EO, July 17, 1920. LIES— EO, April 10, 1920; EO April 20, 1918; EO, Sept. 20, 1918; Summer Annual, 1923, 69. LIFE— EO, Nov. 18, 1911; EO, Sept. 11, 1920; EO, April 25, 1914; EO, Sept. 13, 1913; EO, Oct. 2, 1920; EO, Aug. 20, 1921; EO, May 17, 1913; EO, Oct. 11, 1919; EO, Sept. 1, 1917; EO, Dec. 21, 1912; EO, Feb. 11, 1911; EO, May 12, 1919; Summer Annual, 1923, 1. LONELINESS— EO, Dec. 8, 1917; Summer Annual, 1923, 79. LOVE— EO, Nov. 24, 1917; Summer Annual, 1923, 73; EO, Dec. 11, 1915; Summer Annual, 1923, 51; EO, Dec. 20, 1913; EO, Dec. 20, 1913; EO, Oct. 2, 1920; Summer Annual, 1923, 84; EO, May 22, 1915; EO

121

Feb. 22, 1919.

MARRIAGE— EO, Sept. 22, 1917; EO, Aug. 23, 1919; EO, Aug. 28, 1915; EO, June 29, 1918; EO, March 6, 1920; EO, April 30, 1921; EO, Sept. 7, 1912; EO, Dec. 4, 1909; EO, Feb. 17, 1917; EO, April 20, 1912; EO, Nov. 21 1914; EO, May 22, 1915; EO, Oct. 23, 1915; EO, Jan. 13, 1912; EO, June 27, 1914; Summer Annual, 1923, 64; EO, May 23, 1914; EO, Dec. 2, 1916; EO, March 6, 1920; Summer Annual, 1923, 56; EO, Dec. 20, 1913; EO, May 22, 1915; EO, Feb. 10, 1912; EO, Oct. 5, 1912; EO, Aug. 23, 1919; Summer Annual, 1923, 36; EO, March 23, 1912; EO, Nov. 24, 1917; EO, July 20, 1918; EO, Oct. 13, 1917. MEEKNESS— EO, Sept. 16, 1916. MEN— EO, Jan. 25, 1919; EO, March 5, 1910; EO, March 30, 1917; EO, March 20, 1920; EO, June 6, 1914; EO, Feb. 7, 1919; Summer Annual, 1923, 66; EO, April 20, 1918; EO, April 6, 1912; Summer Annual, 1923, 56; EO, July 17, 1920; EO, Jan. 25, 1919; EO, May 4, 1912. MISFORTUNE— EO, June 18, 1910; EO, Dec. 12, 1914; EO, June 12, 1915; EO, May 11, 1918; EO, May 6, 1916; EO, May 6, 1916; EO, Nov. 1, 1919; EO, April 5, 1919; EO, June 6, 1914; EO, June 8, 1912; EO, June 6, 1914; EO, Dec. 20, 1913; Summer Annual, 1923, 90; EO, Sept. 1, 1917; EO, Oct. 23, 1920; Summer Annual, 1923, 52. MORALITY— EO, Jan. 22, 1921; EO, May 25, 1918; Summer Annual, 1920, 36; EO, Dec. 6, 1913; EO, Feb. 26, 1916; EO, Jan. 27, 1917; EO, March 24, 1913; Summer Annual, 1923, 39; EO, Nov. 22, 1919; Summer Annual, 1923, 60; Summer Annual, 1922, 39; Summer Annual, 1923, 85; Summer Annual, 1923, 54; EO, Aug. 26, 1911. MOURNING— EO, Jan. 22, 1921. MUSIC— EO, Dec. 4, 1909; EO, Aug. 23, 1919; EO, Nov. 1, 1919.

NEWSPAPERMEN— EO ,Dec. 11, 1915. NEIGHBORS— EO, Nov. 24, 1917; EO, Sept. 22, 1917; EO, Dec. 6, 1919; EO, April 10, 1920; Summer Annual, 1923, 64; EO, March 30, 1917; EO, Nov. 19, 1921.

OPPORTUNITY— Summer Annual, 1922, 47; EO, Sept. 22, 1917. OPTIMISM— EO, Feb. 7, 1919; EO, June 3, 1911; ORIGINALITY— EO, Nov. 20, 1915.

PATIENCE— EO, Oct. 19, 1912; EO, Dec. 11, 1915. PERFORMANCE — EO, May 22, 1915; Summer Annual, 1923, 56; EO, Feb. 7, 1919. PERSUASION— EO, Nov. 22, 1919; EO, Nov. 20, 1915; PESSIMISM — EO, Oct. 19, 1912; EO, Aug. 2, 1913. PLAY— EO, Sept.

21, 1918. POLITICS— EO, Oct. 19, 1912; EO, March 14, 1914; EO, March 9, 1918; EO, Nov. 16, 1912; Summer Annual, 1922, 33; EO, Feb. 8, 1919; EO, Dec. 20, 1919; EO, Oct. 8, 1921; EO, Dec. 2, 1916; EO, Aug. 28, 1920; EO, March 20, 1920; EO, July 29, 1922; Summer Annual, 1922, 51; EO, Sept. 1, 1917; EO, April 19, 1919; EO, Nov. 19, 1921; EO, Oct. 19, 1918. POPULAR OPINION— EO, March 6, 1920. POPULARITY— EO, Aug. 3, 1912; EO, April 8, 1916; EO, May 22, 1915; EO, March 20, 1915; EO, March 20, 1920. POVERTY— EO, Oct. 23, 1920; EO, April 25, 1914; EO, Dec. 12, 1914; EO, Sept. 22, 1917; EO, Oct. 19, 1912; EO, April 19, 1919; EO, Dec. 11, 1915; EO, Jan. 25, 1919; Summer Annual, 1923, 60; EO, March 20, 1915. PRIDE— EO, May 22, 1915; EO, June 12, 1915; EO, Nov. 21, 1914. PROHIBITION— EO, July 8, 1916; EO, Jan. 25, 1919; EO, May 22, 1915. PRUDES— Summer Annual, 1923, 62.

RELIGION— EO, April 30, 1921; EO, May 22, 1915; EO, Dec. 6, 1913; EO, Dec. 12, 1914; EO, Feb. 25, 1905; Summer Annual, 1923, 14; EO, April 8, 1916. REMORSE— EO, Dec. 20, 1919. REPUTATION— EO, Jan. 27, 1912; EO, May 13, 1922.

SADNESS— EO, Aug. 23, 1919; EO, Aug. 9, 1919. SARCASM— EO, May 11, 1918; EO, Aug. 23, 1919; EO, Nov. 16, 1912. SAVINGS— EO, March 15, 1919. SIN— EO, Nov. 20, 1915; EO, Oct. 19, 1912; EO, Feb. 21, 1920; EO, March 30, 1918; EO, Feb. 2, 1918; EO, Sept. 13, 1919. SPECULATION— EO, Feb. 10, 1912. SPEECH— EO, April 30, 1921. SPINSTERS— EO, Aug. 14, 1920; EO, Oct. 2, 1920; EO, Nov. 3, 1917. STUPIDITY— EO, Oct. 23, 1915; EO, July 26, 1919; EO, April 30, 1921; EO, April 25, 1914; EO, July 29, 1922; EO, Feb. 5, 1921; EO, June 29, 1918. SUCCESS— EO, May 6, 1916; EO, July 3, 1915; Summer Annual, 1924, 52; EO, Feb. 26, 1916; EO, June 6, 1914; EO, Sept. 7, 1912; EO, Nov. 24, 1917. SUSPICION— EO, Jan. 27, 1917; Summer Annual, 1923, 60; EO, Nov. 3, 1917; Summer Annual, 1923, 81; EO, Nov. 11, 1916; Summer Annual, 1923, 85; EO, Dec. 6, 1919.

TEARS— EO, Oct. 19, 1912; EO, Oct. 19, 1912; Summer Annual, 1921, 57. TELEPHONES— EO, March 9, 1918; EO, March 20, 1915. TEMPTATION— EO, June 11, 1921; EO, Dec. 30, 1911; EO, March 14, 1914; EO, Jan. 27, 1917; EO, March 20, 1920; EO, Nov. 22, 1919. THRIFT— EO, Sept. 1, 1917. TIME— Summer Annual, 1920, 33. TROUBLE— Summer Annual, 1920, 60; EO, Sept. 3, 1919.

TRUTH— EO, May 31, 1919; EO, Nov. 16, 1912; EO, March 14, 1914; EO, Oct. 19, 1912; EO, April 3, 1915; EO, Jan. 25, 1919; EO, March 20, 1915; EO, June 11, 1921.

VANITY— EO, Sept. 1, 1920; EO, Aug. 28, 1920, VICE— EO, May 8, 1915; EO, June 5, 1920; EO, Jan. 27, 1912; EO, June 28, 1919; EO, Oct. 13, 1917. VINDICTIVENESS— Summer Annual, 1921, 54; EO, April 8, 1916; EO, Feb. 11, 1911; Summer Annual, 1921, 54. VOLUBILITY— EO, Feb. 19, 1921; EO, Feb. 5, 1921; EO, Dec. 12, 1914; EO, Nov. 18, 1911; EO, May 31, 1919; EO, April 25, 1914; EO, Aug. 14, 1920; EO, April 3, 1915; EO, Feb. 10, 1912; EO, April 19, 1919; EO, Nov. 8, 1913; EO, Nov. 22, 1919; EO, May 18, 1912; EO, Oct. 23, 1920; EO, May 23, 1914; Summer Annual, 1923, 87.

WEALTH— EO, May 17, 1913; EO, Feb. 5, 1921; EO, Oct. 13, 1917; EO, Aug. 26, 1911; Summer Annual, 1923, 64; EO, Sept. 16, 1911; EO, Aug. 2, 1913; EO, May 27, 1916. WEATHER— EO, May 22, 1915. WHISKEY— EO, June 5, 1920; EO, Nov. 1, 1919; Summer Annual, 1923, 25; EO, Nov. 18, 1911. WISDOM— EO, May 22, 1915; EO, April 30, 1921; EO, Oct. 19, 1912; EO, Aug. 9, 1919; EO, Oct. 2, 1920; EO, Nov. 22, 1919; EO, Dec. 20, 1913; EO, Feb. 8, 1919; EO, June 29, 1918; EO, Dec. 11, 1920; EO, Dec. 11, 1915; Summer Annual, 1923, 70; EO, Oct. 14, 1916; EO, Nov. 20, 1915; EO, July 29, 1922. WOMEN— EO, March 18, 1916; EO, April 20, 1918; EO, Oct. 19, 1918; EO, Jan. 22, 1921; Summer Annual, 1924, 61; Summer Annual, 1923, 61; EO, Oct. 23, 1920; EO, Jan. 13, 1912; EO, Nov. 3, 1917; EO, Oct. 8, 1921; EO, May 11, 1918; EO, Dec. 3, 1921; EO, Oct. 19, 1912; EO, Nov. 20, 1915; EO, Dec. 15, 1917; EO, Oct. 5, 1912; EO, Feb. 26, 1916; EO, Dec. 15, 1917. WOMEN'S SUFFRAGE— EO, March 18, 1916; EO, May 6, 1911; EO, March 2, 1915; EO, Sept. 22, 1917; EO, Dec. 11, 1915. WORK— EO, Sept. 13, 1919. WORRY— EO, July 29, 1922; EO, May 12, 1919.

DESIGNED BY
DAVID JOHN SHAW
TYPESET BY
DARHALL TYPESETTING LIMITED
PRINTED & BOUND BY
T. H. BEST COMPANY

1976